To
Begin
Again

Also by M. F. K. Fisher

M.F.K. Fisher

To

Begin

Again

Stories and Memoirs,
1908–1929

Pantheon Books
New York and San Francisco

Originally published in hardcover by Pantheon Books in 1992.

Some of the essays included in this work were originally published in the following
publications: *The American Way, Architectural Digest, Arts and Antiques, California
Magazine, Food and Wine, Gastronomy, Gourmet, Negative Capabilities, The New
Yorker, The Occidental, San Francisco Magazine* and *Westways.*

Grateful acknowledgment is made to the following for permission to reprint previously
published material:
North Point Press: "I Chose Chicken à la King" by M.F.K. Fisher, originally published
in *Among Friends,* 1983.
University of California Press: "Ridicklus" by M.F.K. Fisher, originally published in
State of the Language; 1990 Edition, edited by Leonard Michaels and
Christopher Ricks.
Weldon Russell Pty. Ltd.: "The First Kitchen" by M.F.K. Fisher, originally published
in *The Cook's Room* (published in the United States by HarperCollins, 1990).

Library of Congress Cataloging-in-Publication Data
Fisher, M.F.K. (Mary Frances Kennedy), 1908–1992.
To begin again : stories and memoirs, 1908–1929 / M.F.K. Fisher.
p.   cm.
ISBN 0-679-75082-7
1. Fisher, M.F.K., (Mary Frances Kennedy), 1908–1992 — Biography.
2. Authors, American — 20th century — Biography.   3. Food writers — United
States — Biography.   I. Title.
PS3511.I7428Z469   1992
641'.092 — dc20
[B]   92-54113
CIP

Book design by Cheryl Cipriani
Manufactured in the United States of America
First Paperback Edition
2   4   6   8   9   7   5   3   1

Contents

To
Begin
Again

EDITOR'S NOTE

The timespan covered by each essay is indicated by the date(s) following its title. Dates at the end of essays indicate when they were written.

To Begin

I find increasingly as I grow older that I do not consider myself a writer. A writer to me is someone who spends much of his adult life developing a certain way of using a language, and this becomes his *style*. Usually, if he is any good at it, other people will admire and imitate it.

I have not done this, even unconsciously. But by now people sometimes refer to me as a stylist, or they talk about my style, and I think this is because of my habit of putting words onto paper as much as possible as I say them in talking or telling. I have always tried to speak clearly—that is, to make what I am saying clear and logical to the listener or reader . . . and, of course, to make it interesting if the story itself is interesting. But I do not try to tell it in *my* way.

Unfortunately or not, my way, since I was aware at all of trying to catch whatever attention possible, has been both direct and as dramatic as I could make it. Since the beginning of my talking years, my family has teasingly warned me and other gullible listeners that I never spoil a story by sticking to the truth. This is a plain lie, because I do not lie. But I have never seen any reason to be dull, and since I was less than four I have enjoyed entertaining and occasionally startling anyone who may be listening.

The first time I was aware of the heady powers of creating and then holding an audience was when I was a little past three. We were staying in a rented "bungalow" on the palisades in Santa Monica, California. Father was scouting for a small newspaper to buy, since my parents had decided that they could no longer drift on the money from the sale of half of the *Albion* (Michigan) *Recorder* to his brother Walter, and I was taking my morning stroll with a maid or somebody while Mother stayed home with my baby sister Anne.

The palisades then held a long single stretch of posh winter houses for rather affluent midwesterners, so we were doubtless visiting some of Mother's relatives. Across the street from the houses and along the top of the high cliffs was a kind of park, planted with exotic palms and cactuses and generously supplied with benches for its elderly late-Victorian clientele. Sturdy fences of driftwood protected us landward from the rare carriages and even rarer automobiles on the wide street, and seaward they kept us from toppling down several hundred feet onto the rocky Pacific shoreline. This oddly dusty parkway may still be there, but more likely it is covered by high-rise condominiums for the very affluent descendants of those well-to-do midwesterners.

On this particular day in about 1911, when I was brought back from my morning stroll, I told my mother—along with other reports on things like hurting my finger on a cactus needle and falling down twice—that I had seen a man fall out of a brown box up in the sky and turn over and over, until there was the ocean.

Mother scolded me crossly, as I am sure I remember, about

making up silly stories. At lunch, though, she thought it amusing enough to repeat to my father, perhaps as proof that I was learning to speak almost too well. And he looked oddly at her and at me and then said, "She may make a good reporter. Eyewitness story." Mother looked very sad, and said, "Oh, dear! Oh, mercy," and he told her that a crazy daredevil had taken his flying machine up over the bay and suddenly jumped out, with no parachute, no nothing. The plane had gone further out to sea and then dived. "Oh, dear," Mother said, and then said something very brisk and meaningful to Father about forgetting all about it because there was no use letting little girls imagine things, was there?

And from then on, in a tacit family plot, everything that I said was taken with a grain or two of salt. If I came home from school and announced after lunch (for from the beginning we never mentioned politics, money, or trouble before dessert had been served) that I had seen a dead cat at the corner of Friends and Philadelphia, small smiles of amused disbelief would flicker around the table, and the grown-ups would settle back visibly, ready for another of my lurid reports. If I said something terse like, "Well, that's all," they would lead me on. If I said, "It was just lying there, dead," Father or even Grandmother Holbrook would ask gently, "Are you sure?" or "How did you know?" And I'd be fool enough to go on. "Well, Garland Swain and I were going to run across Philadelphia before Mr. Trueblood backed out of his barn in his Franklin, and suddenly this little kitten—"

"Black, striped, or what?" Father would interrupt.

"This little striped gray kitten scooted out from in back of the Friends' Church, and another car, not Mr. Trueblood's, appeared almost without a sound and speeded up when it saw us starting to run across the street. And *suddenly* . . ." And I was off. I wanted to please my audience while I had them caught. Sometimes I managed to hold them, and often I did not, so that I quickly grew wise about crowd reaction and attention span and all the things that people now learn in college courses about writing and acting.

But the plain truth is that I did not ever lie; I may have stretched things a tiny bit, here and there, but I never said that people were there who weren't (Garland Swain and I were going to meet Tolbert Moorhead *after* we crossed the street), and never did I embroider the real action in any drama (Mr. Trueblood's car did *not* hit either the kitten or the other automobile, which could not help giving the poor creature a glancing blow that knocked it a few feet into some bushes—and here I could have embroidered freely, but instead I began to cry because it was so shocking to see something so lively suddenly turn limp and still).

I begin to remember now about that time I saw the little cat die. I begin to wonder why I mentioned it to my family at all, for surely I knew that it was not something any of us would like to hear about after lunch. Probably I meant firmly *not* to mention it?

—*1992*

1
Native Truths
(1908–1952)

I don't know why I've always felt embarrassed when I have to admit that I'm not a native Californian. People tell me that I'm silly, and really I cannot say why I feel the way I do about this apparently delicate question of where I was born.

The truth is that I was born in Albion, Michigan, on July 3, 1908. I still know some people there and some who come from there, and all of them are good 'uns. This minute, for instance, there is a man who is the curator of an outfit called the Albion Historical Society who writes occasionally to me as if we knew each other, and I not only like but admire and respect him. In fact, everything I know about Albion is good—except perhaps that I wish I'd not been born there!

Any place over the California border would have done for me, from Oregon down through Nevada, Arizona, and on south toward Mexico, locally known as Baja. I'd have preferred to be born in Mexico (Baja), of course, because I've always hated being pink instead of brown. That, my own mother assured me regretfully when I was about seven, was and is my fate. I am pink indeed and forever, and what is worse, I am not a native Californian.

In Albion I was born in the upstairs bedroom of a house that was shared with my Uncle Walter and his bride. My father Rex and his bride Edith lived on the second floor.

This whole adventure of being born is apocryphal, of course, and I am told that an old lady came across the street in the heat wave that preceded and followed my birth and said firmly to my mother, "This child won't live through the week."

"Why not?" my mother asked, probably with languor (although my birth had been an easy one), and the old woman replied that anyone could tell that I was not long for this world because my new little fingers lay loosely spread open on my stomach and "healthy babies' fists are clenched." Then she questioned Mother about why I was named Mary Frances. "It seems strange to me," she sniffed. "And your mother is such a Christian woman, too. I thought you would surely name her something from the Bible." Mother probably closed her eyes in boredom at this obvious non sequitur.

More apocrypha: Father got his fellow volunteers from the Albion Fire Department to spray the hot walls of the bedroom, which meant that he would treat them later to an ice cream and beer party. When I was five days old, I was taken for a ride with Rex in the town's first automobile, although now it is not clear whether it was a Willys-Knight or a Stutz. Mother consigned us both to hell or heaven and shuddered gently when Father confessed later that we had gone forty-two miles per hour.

So . . . we did come to California by the time I was somewhat less than three, and naturally I do not blame my poor parents for preferring to have me in Albion, Michigan, before they headed like

helpless lemmings toward the Pacific Ocean and whatever freedom
they could find there. They managed to stay in Michigan until my
sister Anne was born two years after I was, and then to everyone's
astonishment, including theirs, they simply pulled up stakes.

My father Rex Kennedy, a fourth-generation newspaperman,
refused categorically to continue to be one. He sold his half-interest
in the *Albion Recorder* to his older brother Walter. He took the
boodle and literally ran westward, with two little babies and a shy,
proud, asocial, snobbish woman, his wife and my mother Edith
Oliver Holbrook. Rex decided he would be a geologist probably
. . . possibly . . . maybe. Mother, who was literally a prairie princess, a Daisy Miller indeed, whose shy manners were always taken
as aloof pride, and who was one of the most conservative people I
myself ever knew, followed her husband Rex without anything but
obvious pleasure. And the four of us were undoubtedly among the
first beatniks of the Far West—unwittingly, of course.

Because of Mother's background we headed toward money
and security, toward an island in Puget Sound then owned totally
by a rich uncle, one of her father's vaguely bankerish brothers. But
because of Rex himself, we rented a deserted cabin across the bay
from the rich relatives' island. Rex had a rowboat, and probably
when Edith needed a bath or some other touch of real elegance,
he would row her over to the island. Mostly though, we lived in
stately but dingy bliss in the little cabin. Every day Father rowed
out into the Sound, and when there was a log of exotic wood like
teak or mahogany that had cut loose or been cut from a raft of
wood towed by Japanese freighters, he would tie it to the back of
his rowboat and bring it back to shore. There he would either
chop it into crude furniture for the cabin or sell it to a dealer in
fine furniture. In other words, my father was a scavenger. And we
lived on the money he made from his piracy, plus an occasional

dip into the money from the sale of his half of the *Recorder,* until finally he and Edith decided that they had better try ranching instead of beachcombing.

We headed toward California then, and I was three years old in Ventura, where we lived for some five months about a hundred feet from the foggy beach. I often heard later from Edith that Anne and I barked like seals for at least the first few months we were there until finally a Mexican neighbor, probably in desperation, gave Mother her recipe for cough syrup (and here it is). Take equal parts of honey, glycerin, and fresh lemon juice, and beat them well together. Keep in a little bottle, and take a small slow swig as needed for coughs.

Ventura loomed in our after-dinner conversations as we all grew up (by "all" I mean that we were soon joined by a new sister and brother and of course by countless friends and relatives), and more often than not we sat around after dinner at the table, taking what we referred to as our White Wine Trips. These Trips may have been hard on the wine cellar, but they were always good for us. Edith sometimes withdrew to the nearest couch, convinced that nobody could discuss a thing without arguing, and she was deathly afraid of arguments. Discussions were very different, we all assured her, and we went on talking amiably for many years on the Trips.

And more often than not, at least when topics became thin or dull, we'd wonder what our lives would have been like if Rex had not turned in his option on the faltering, half-dead little orange grove he had determined to buy. The story is that a few hours before the option was going to be up, he decided to buy a shovel and dig around the roots of one of his future gold mines, because as a former farm boy he had begun to wonder why his orange trees had never grown more than an inch in some three years or so— and a few feet below the surface he hit hardpan! He ran for what was left of his option just in time, and he and Edith and their two formerly coughing brats (*and* magic cough syrup) headed for San Diego. They were dead broke by then.

Rex bowed to fate and took a job as city editor of a big daily paper. It must have been miserable for both my parents. I don't remember anything about it—although I am sure I do have one clear memory of my life on Puget Sound, when I was down at the bottom of the beached rowboat pretending to save all our lives by dipping some of the bilge water out with a little tin cup. My six-month-old sister Anne lay on her blanket. My mother always insisted that I could not possibly recall this too-early memory, but she was mistaken there. It is still clear and full to me.

Now all I have of Ventura is the Mexican recipe and a feeling of great solace that Rex did not become a multimillionaire from the oil that was discovered just under the hardpan a few weeks after we fled the place. And of San Diego I remember nothing at all! Later I was told that Rex loathed having a boss and that he and Edith were pretty miserable down there, but the real reason they left was the fleas.

In 1911 San Diego was believed to be the West Coast Port of the Future, and it was already a thriving, filthy place, a home for every wandering flea from the Far East. And Rex Kennedy, until he was about thirty-two, was chemically attractive to fleas—as he was always to men, women, and children—so that after the paper was put to bed, midafternoon, he'd stagger home, increasingly wan and thin and listless and probably proportionately cranky. Edith would brush him down on the sidewalk, and he would then run to the bathroom and jump into the empty tub, while she took all his clothes and shook them out in the backyard. And the tub would be hopping with the bugs that fell from him, and eventually he'd go flealess but sick as a dog to bed. It must have been a hell of a life in every way: they were both fastidious people. Finally a doctor said that Rex must get out of town that minute or die. (I can vouch for this whole sad story because until I was thirty-two years old I, too, carried the same chemistry and could not walk through the lobby of the St. Francis Hotel in San Francisco or even the Paris Ritz without collecting at least fourteen fleas. And the last time I lived in Mexico I, too, staggered home to California with what my horrified doctor called the worst case of flea bites he'd ever seen. There were 147 of them, and he said that if I'd had 150 I'd be dead.)

And the next thing I remember is being in Whittier watching my mother put my baby sister Anne into the top drawer of a hotel bureau. We stayed at the Pickering Hotel until my father bought the biggest available house in town from Mr. Myers, the department store owner. Of course the house was not ostentatious because it was built by and for the Quakers who made up the town. There were less than five thousand original Quaker settlers in Whittier then, and we swelled the ranks of the so-called gentiles by four, which made us almost one hundred in number. Naturally, Grandmother Holbrook financed the purchase of the big house, while Rex and Edith Kennedy filled it with more siblings for Anne and me and a steady stream of relatives. (In those days, people stayed for months instead of one night or two, and there were always a few semipermanent "visitors," all of them fascinating and half of them as batty as June bugs.)

Rex (and Grandmother Holbrook, of course) bought the *Whittier News,* a small daily of ill repute, which no decent Quaker would operate. It was tacitly understood that Father would either leave or be pushed out in one year. We were definitely gentiles, as well as genteel, to the Quaker settlers, and we were always a puzzlement because of Rex's superb training as a newspaperman and also because we were decent people despite our lack of even a faint hint of the "friendly persuasion." We stayed on for some forty-two years, and both my mother and my father were genuinely mourned after they died by every sect, including the one that had most disapproved of us at the beginning.

Although I am quite sure I remember my little sister in the bureau drawer at the Pickering Hotel, my first really keen memory of being there in Whittier, and forever and happily, too, was the day we moved into 115 North Painter Avenue. The little patch of grass in the front yard was dry and brown, as it was perforce in front of every house on our long block, and I stood looking through a scraggly privet hedge and another little girl almost as old as I stared pleasantly back at me as she masturbated. I looked curiously at her for a while, and then I went along unmoved to watch men struggle to bring Mother's piano and all the other things into the mysterious new building that was at once our home. That night Mother told me seriously that she hoped I would never do what little Ruth had been doing to herself because it would make me nervous, and I wondered what on earth she was talking about and why she thought I would try to copy anybody.

The Painter Avenue house was a fine place, indeed, and for many years. I was a completely happy person there, I think. Life rolled on and I learned constantly and eagerly. Everything was exciting to me. I never wondered whether people liked me, but I know as I look back that I had many good friends.

And in 1920 when we moved from Painter Avenue down onto a small orange ranch on what was called Painter Extension—when Mother was through producing her last batch of children and my brother David was not yet a year old—I was still a very happy child. I stayed this way, excited and enraptured by everything and especially by the new life in "the country," for at least three or four more years. But then everything crashed and I became completely adolescent and so disagreeable that Edith Kennedy, who had always been dependent upon me for my cheery usefulness to her with my siblings, wanted me out of the house and insisted that I go away to school when I was sixteen.

We always returned to the Ranch, though, as long as Father and Mother were alive, no matter how widely the whole family roamed. By now that "country" no longer exists, any more than the happy child does.

I still feel embarrassed that I was not born a native Californian because I truly think I am one. I really started to be me somewhere there between the old Pickering Hotel and 115 North Painter. My sister did sleep first in a bureau drawer until we could move, and I did indeed watch Ruthie solemnly as she played with herself, also solemnly, and I do feel "native." So pooh! to all my friends who look at me pityingly when I confess that I was not born in Santa Monica or La Jolla or Montecito but that I sprang full-blown at the age of three into a real native life here. My first sights of this new world are perhaps more vivid than they would have been to a newborn child, but I feel that I was that, and of course I don't remember my own impressions of this world when I emerged in Albion, Michigan, so perhaps I should be thankful that I was three instead of newborn as I stood there on the dry grass of our little patch of lawn in 1911.

—1989

Author's Note: We left the house forever in 1952 after Rex died. It was bulldozed and made into a park for children and old people.

2
On
Coveting
(1912)

While I don't think I am a covetous person, I do remember the first thing I ever thought that I had to have, which I suppose is a form of coveting.

There was a little shop on the Pike in Long Beach where I spent two weeks once in the spring of 1912, when I was three years old going on four. Father was trying to ready a home for us in Whittier, and through my Grandmother Holbrook, who was to live with us for the next eight years or so, we rented a little apartment in Long Beach.

My younger sister Anne and I went there with my mother, who seemed to spend most of her time in bed with what was called a Sick Headache, which was probably a form of migraine or perhaps merely shock at the prospect of continuing her life as a middle-class American woman in one more small town. Whatever the cause, we seldom saw her and instead spent long happy days with a series of faceless and probably witless missionary friends of my grandmother, who was a famous Christian woman from Iowa and one of the uncrowned queens of Long Beach, in those far days when the Iowa picnic was the social event of the year. In fact, anything from Iowa was magic in that town, or so it seemed to us, and Grandmother's name opened many doors that the old lady never suspected.

Who would think, for instance, that the name of the un-crowned queen would act like a magic wand in a little Japanese shop on the Pike? I remember that the first day we were in Long Beach the ancient missionary who was on duty to take care of Mrs. Holbrook's grandchildren led us at once to the little shop owned by Mr. Ishizawa. It was among the poorer and junkier of all the poor and junky little shops owned by Orientals on the quiet strip that was laid like a ribbon along the beach. Mr. Ishizawa bowed and smiled constantly, and his bows became even deeper when he learned that we were indeed Mrs. Holbrook's grandchildren. Probably he was told that the missionary had known his father in Japan, or some such Christianlike fable.

But whatever the charm was, it worked, and when we left that first day, and then every day thereafter for the next two weeks, we were given a little gift by Mr. Ishizawa himself. After the second or third day, the current missionary permitted us to choose our own presents, but with strict instructions for us never to choose anything beyond the ten-cent shelf. This, though, contained many mysterious and beautiful things: tiny dolls made of white plaster with cotton kimonos wrapped around them and little red mouths and slanting black eyes painted on their very white faces, and even smaller bottles of sandalwood perfume, which Mother did not care to have us open near her, and little handkerchiefs painted with kimonos and Mount Fuji, which she did allow to be laid on her pillow by her head. And there were little cakes of soap shaped like obscene pink Kewpies, which we did not like at all but which were thought to be more proper for American children to love than the Japanese dolls that we preferred.

Best of all there were sticks of joss incense. They were, of course, forbidden for us ever to light, except when Father came down from Whittier. Then Anne and I would lie in our bed that pulled down from behind the couch in the living room of the grim little apartment and listen to Mother and Father talking and laughing in the sudden warmth and beauty of the weekend, with the smell of the incense burning. And the next day we knew was the one when Father took us to the Pike alone, while Mother waited for his return and then took to her bed again.

Sunday was a great day, with everyone jostling and happy and the many sailors with their girls and the sound of rifles popping in all the shooting galleries and the steady shrieks that came from the roller coaster.

The first Sunday Mr. Ishizawa smiled at us when we passed by. The second and last Sunday, we went into his shop, and I saw the one thing that I was to covet for the rest of my life. It was not on the familiar ten-cent shelf but in another part of the small shop. I suppose I could have bought one myself later on, but it never occurred to me to do so. It seemed too bad, almost tragic, but it was plainly something of great value, especially in those first far days when it was inconceivable that I would someday have the money of my own to spend on anything I wanted. It was the Unobtainable Jewel to me then, and it still is.

This jewel was a tiny piece of carved coral, shaped like a little rose, probably the size of my thumbnail when I was almost four. It was hung on a tiny gold chain. Probably it cost something insurmountable, like fifty cents or five dollars. Anyway, it was much more than the dime I was to use as my one familiar coin for several more years. If a dime could buy a doll, or three sticks of incense, or even a tiny bottle of sandalwood perfume that my mother would not let us put on with the little silk handkerchiefs with Mount Fuji painted on them, what need was there for any other coin?

Yet I knew enough that I should not ask for the little coral rose, for Mr. Ishizawa would surely have given it to me with a small smile and bow, and that would have displeased my mother and father, and the magic spell would have been broken forever. Of course, never again could ten cents buy as much as it did then in those days when my Grandmother's name had a special charm to it. Never were there such beautiful dolls sold for a dime to any children anywhere, and never, I know, has a little piece of coral, tinted by hand in Italy to look like a tiny rose and then copied by skilled Oriental fingers to sell for one-tenth its real value, been so alluring, so forbidden.

The complexity of this small new obsession of mine was mixed with a strange Christian ethic, probably—something mysterious that flowed between our missionary companions and the little Japanese merchant on the Long Beach Pike. And the rose was an emblem of the unobtainable, and one that I could easily have asked for and perhaps got in the next seventy-five years or so.

Once, I remember, I went to a place near Naples where these roses were as common as the grains of sand along the shore. I still felt the magic of their tiny perfect little petals and knew that no matter how much they cost or how little, they were beyond any price I could pay. I see one now and know just as surely that I could ask for it and wear it myself, but I would never do that. Mr. Ishizawa would come in my dreams and take it away.

—1990

3
Tree Change
(1912–1929)

Sometimes the spirit of Christmas seems nothing more than a conditioned reflex, and it is hard to make it work successfully when the calendar calls it up. There must be children in it.

I am sure that my own feelings about the festival are, after many decades, still dictated by the basically Germanic ideas fed to me as a child: "O Tannenbaum" and "Silent Night"; a jolly fat man with a red nose, a wonderful uniform of scarlet to match that nose and white to match his beard; presents long planned for and worked upon—hideous pincushions stitched with yarn at school for a secret special gift to Mother and later a clay ashtray glazed in purple and mustard for our all-forgiving father.

The tree was essential, in my family, in spite of the disapproval of our austere grandmother, who felt that it was pagan nonsense. Occasionally she sat through all this un-Christian foolery, casting a firm if futile pall over it, but often she went away somewhere (where? perhaps back to Battle Creek or to a convention of Campbellites in Asbury, New Jersey), and then we indulged in rich dishes, butter cookies, candies from relatives in Pittsburgh, probably in direct proportion to the miles between our stern matriarch and ourselves.

My younger sister was usually bilious by Christmas Day and lay languidly on the couch by the fire while we brought her countless packages. She was a secret eater and used to hunt out and devour large caches of festival bakings that Mother and the cook-of-the-moment had believed to be well hidden.

I now know that her need to punish herself and all of us by this compulsive gluttony and its results was an indication of how she would die, some fifty years later. Then, though, it was simply understood beforehand that Anne would have a serious bile attack a day or so before the fiesta and be the center of all our loving attentions on the Day. In a not very funny way, it was part of our traditional trappings.

And the tree twinkled, and all our hearts were full of true happiness, even if some of our livers were in protest at the seasonal flood of delicious generous bakings and roastings, all unthought of while Grandmother was in residence. Green pastures!

The first Christmas I remember was the best one, probably because it was the most innocent one in my life. I was four, and it was our first year in Whittier. My sister Anne was two, and it was arranged that we would get into bed with Father, on the sleeping porch upstairs, while mother was at early service singing in the choir. We lay there waiting for the bugler to climb up to the steeple of the Friends' Church and play "Joy to the World! The Lord is Come." It was something special to wait for, and we were trembling with excitement because Father told us it would be beautiful.

We loved being in bed with Father, too. The sleeping porch

was like a bird's nest, high at the back of the tall house. Father was a big man, and warm, and we lay on either side of him and felt his long arms around us in the cold dark waiting for the sounds to come.

They began just as the sun rose on Christmas Day. It was still a little dark, and the sound of the trumpet came to us in a wobbling way, played by an old man, Father said. I remember feeling sharply awake, so that when the first notes of a trumpet sounded into the starry air, I cried out something like "YES," and little Anne awoke with a snap on the other side of Father's big chest, and he pulled us closer as we lay listening.

From the top of the square steeple of the Friends' Church, less than two blocks from our warm nest, a man blew the first notes bravely on his horn, sometimes trembling and flatting a little. First he played to the north. Then he blew to the east, where we lay breathless with the mysterious, triumphant beauty of the sound, and to the south, where in a few years we would move. Then he sounded his tiny blast westward, toward the great Pacific.

Father knew the words: "Joy to the world! The Lord is come." When the trumpet finally ended its announcement, he sang on softly, "And heaven and nature sing!"

Then Mother came running in, all cool-cheeked and laughing, and then we were in our Sunday dresses at a special breakfast with candles on the table and probably muffins or sausages for a treat, and *finally* we went into the living room. (I knew there was more to this day, but what?)

At the end of the long dark living room was a hole in the wall for the door to an apartment we were going to build for Grandmother, who was soon coming to live with us. The hole had been an ugly fireplace with a gas log that Mother had been very scornful about, so that very soon we were going to build another good decent fireplace on the other wall, the one to the south end of the living room. Now, in front of the hole, which was covered with a blanket to keep out the Christmas chill, there was a low table and on it were two trees, one for my little sister Anne and one for me!

They were about three feet tall. Of course, we knew that they were to go on either side of our new front steps in the next day or so. They were shaped just like Christmas trees and were some kind of pine, I suppose, set in sturdy pine tubs that had roughly braided bands of bamboo peelings around the tops and bottoms. They had been given to Mother and Father by Mr. One. He was a Chinese merchant on the plaza in Los Angeles, and he liked Mother and Father and they liked him. (F. Suey One was a tall man for a Chinese. I did not know that then, because I thought all men were tall because my father was.)

The table was a kitchen table with two fat-bellied drawers, one for sugar and one for flour—a kind of table that was common then when flour and sugar were used more than they are now. Father had found it secondhand in a junkyard and had cut off the legs, and now Anne had her own drawer for crayons and whatever she wanted in this world, and I had my own drawer, and we never thought of looking in each others'.

But the magic part of it was that on that day two little trees stood on it, one for each of us, and each one had a star on top, I remember, glistening and gleaming in the dim room. There was some tinsel, too, and there were a few presents underneath, probably crayons for us both and some coloring books or papers. And they were *our* trees!

The rest of the day I don't remember at all, but we probably ate well. There were many good things about the day for both of us, as there were about all days in those far times, but coming down to find the trees in that long dim room was one of the most innocent and loveliest things that has ever happened to me, I think.

—1978

Author's Note: I got married in September of 1929, but Christmas was always the same while Rex and Edith were alive.

4
A Few Notes About
Aunt Gwen
(1912–1927)

Soon after we began to live in Whittier in 1912, when I was four, we met the Nettleships, a strange family of English medical missionaries who preferred tents to houses. Their daughter became our Aunt Gwen in a wonderful flash, and that summer my little sister Anne and I stayed in their current encampment, under a mighty row of eucalyptus trees a few hundred yards above the sea cliffs south of the village called Laguna. There was a mess tent, and a kitchen with little tents in a square around it, and even a donkey named Noisy to help carry water and supplies. We slept on folding cots, and Aunt Gwen played us songs by Harry Lauder on a little Victrola with a horn, from blue cylinders that we were not to touch.

The next summer, when we drove down from Whittier in the Model-T with a load of camp stuff for the Nettleships, we were horrified to find that someone had built a one-room cabin where our camping place had been. By then, though, Father knew a mysterious old Dutch newspaperman who published a little sheet now and then in Laguna, and from him he learned that the owner of our land wanted to sell the cabin and leave. So Father borrowed $375 and bought the shack and the row of mighty trees on their three vaguely defined township lots, and we went back there every summer for more than twenty-five years, sometimes for four or five months.

Soon after the place was ours, Father and several other Whittier heathens (that is, Episcopalians, non-Quakers) began to add rooms to it. The only one of them who knew beans about building was Uncle Mac, Peter Maclaren, who sang bass in the St. Matthias choir and was a retired Chief Mate on the India run from Glasgow and Liverpool. For about three years, Sundays in summer meant hammers and saws and a picnic, and a caravan of jalopies when we all headed for home at night. Mother usually drove home with some of the other wives and Uncle Mac, and Anne and I snoozed on the backseat of our Ford with the empty beer bottles, while Father headed the parade with a loaded shotgun on the seat beside him, in case the big wildcats in Laguna Canyon got too curious while one of us changed a tire, as often happened in those far times. We never fired the gun but sometimes saw bright eyes blazing in the bushes. Anne and I never felt frightened, but I am not sure about Mother. Gradually she stayed more in Whittier with the new babies.

The Nettleships moved their campgrounds into wilder hills after we found ourselves with a real roof over our heads . . . except for Aunt Gwen, of course, who was our mentor-goddess for the next many years, both in the big solid house in Whittier and in the thrown-together shack at the beach. We lived and ate more casually in Laguna, more carelessly, so that it did not matter that we had only cold running water in the lean-to kitchen. In fact, we felt almost too citified, after bringing water in from the one outside tap for the first couple of years, before Uncle Mac worked some magic with discarded pipe and a faucet. There was a two-burner kerosene stove on wobbly legs, with a tin box we could set over one burner for an oven, and shelves next to the stinking little stove held a few cast-off pots and cups and bowls, trash from all our friends who brought them down on Sundays instead of throwing them away. There was one big iron skillet, which Aunt Gwen used for everything from frying eggs and fish to heating the dishwater. All the china was cracked or chipped. The few kitchen and table tools were shabby and bent. Such things were taken for granted in a beach shack: rejected rocking chairs that tipped over if sat in carelessly, lumpy old quilts, thin mended sheets. It did not matter: we were hungry and healthy, snug with excitement and freedom.

Aunt Gwen, a real Nettleship born in a hammock in a jungle in New Guinea or some such place, was even happier with a campfire than a fancy kerosene stove, and we made a three-stone hearth outside the back door between the kitchen and the outhouse. We heated water there, for a rare bath or for wash day, in a big empty oil can with a wire handle; it had been used so long it hardly tasted of anything but Laguna sulphur. (Water was nasty there, and we seldom drank it.) Father would always bring us old wine jugs full of Whittier tap water on weekends, or now and then we'd have the stuff we could buy for ten cents a jug at a little ranch in Laguna Canyon that also sold cucumbers and tomatoes in the summer. And we had another old oil can that we used to steam mussels in, half full of fresh seaweed over the hot coals. Now and then, for no special reason, Aunt Gwen fried our catch of rock bass out there. It seemed to taste better. . . .

The kitchen stayed the same always, one "thrown up," as Father said when he built anything. (A half-century after he and Uncle Mac and the other middle-aged hoodlums from the St. Matthias Church in Whittier had patched our summer place together, he would still say, "Let's throw up a stone wall round this corner," or "How about throwing up a little fence behind that row of bushes?" It had nothing to do with indigestion, of course, but I've always wondered how a psychiatrist would analyze his innocent phraseology.) A lean-to is never more than a lean-to, and our kitchen, tacked on to the original cabin in Laguna, leaked hopelessly in the winter rains I came to know there when I was grown up. Father never knew this, for summer was forever when he and Uncle Mac were throwing up rooms on three sides of the first house, and the kitchen was part of all the unexpected luxury we felt. It was perhaps eight feet square and had one window looking eastward past the two-holer to the beautiful bare hills and the high horizon that we called the rim of the world. On the north side were the open rickety shelves, with their sad store of rejected dishes and pans, and the two-burner stove with a wide shelf above it for matches and Aunt Gwen's ever-present can of bacon drippings. Under the window, a small wobbly table held current supplies, and dented canisters for sugar and flour, and a beat-up bread box.

On the south wall was an almost surrealistic edifice made jointly, over several summers, by Father and Uncle Mac. It was supposed to be a sink, with two hand-turned and inadequate drainboards on either side, sloping steeply so that the water would run fast off washed dishes. Father had found the little cracked sink in a junkyard, and although the two men devised a kind of outlet for it, there was no running water for several years, and we had to carry a pan or jug of it in from the faucet outside the back door. What made it astonishing, or perhaps merely quaint, was that this spiderlike creation stood almost five feet off the somewhat uneven floor of the kitchen, because Father was six foot five and a half and Mother and Aunt Gwen were both tall women. It did not seem at all strange to me to have to stand on a chair to help Aunt

Gwen with our daily "washing up," and it would never have occurred to any of us to lower it for normal human use. It stood
there for several decades, always with a couple of buckets underneath it to catch whatever might drip down from Uncle Mac's
strange drainboards, or be dropped by people trying to reach its
lofty inadequacies.

On the west wall of this odd little temple to gastronomy, the
heart of the house, THE KITCHEN, there was nothing. I remember leaning against it as I grew older, drying dishes, and probably
Aunt Gwen did, too, but there were no shelves or even graffiti or
cut-out magazine covers on it ever. It was simply the wall of the
old cabin, painted navy blue from the dregs of somebody's leftover
home-done decorating.

Aunt Gwen believed in doing as little as possible inside walls,
so our cooking when we were with her was largely of stuff to put
in our pockets for later. Mornings we ate oranges Father brought
by the crate, because he was interested in the thriving California
citrus industry in those days and got a lot of lagniappes from
ranchers and their packinghouses. There was always toast, made
two slices at a time in a funny arrangement that fitted over one of
the burners, so I thought all toast tasted of kerosene when it was
properly charred on one side and half-done on the other. When
the bread left from weekends got too stale, Aunt Gwen would
soak it in some milk and beaten eggs and fry it in bacon drippings,
and we would sprinkle brown sugar on it for a treat. It was delicious, a genuine *pain perdu*. Then she would fry some bacon, pour
most of its juices back in her can above the stove, and make fried-
egg sandwiches for us to carry greasily in our pockets on our long
treks in every direction of that wild deserted country. (Aunt
Gwen's people were all great walkers, and I remember how
Mother was astonished to learn that long before we knew them,
the Nettleships would spend three or four days carrying their sum-

mer's tents and supplies down from Whittier to the hills of Laguna on foot along the dusty roads and then on their secret trails.)

And when we got home at night, Aunt Gwen fried the fish we had caught, with perhaps some potatoes cut up in their skins and an onion if there was one, always in a good glob from her drippings tin. If there was fresh milk, we had hot cocoa for dessert.

Once I caught a big eel off the rocks near Arch Beach, and Aunt Gwen killed it fast but then made us watch it writhe until sundown, nailed to the back wall of the house. Then she showed me how to skin it and cut it up and help her make a kind of matelote, and it seems strange now that we never associated pain and dying with eating in those innocent and unfeeling days. I hated the death and slow writhings of the water snake and its blood on my hands. But the stew was delicious, the next day for dinner.

Sometimes our goddess made a kind of pone and baked it to a fine stodginess in the little oven set dangerously over one burner. Now and then, for a treat, she would throw in some sugar and raisins and nuts, if there were any.

We seldom ate meat. We walked in to the village every two or three days to get sugar or perhaps a pound of bacon at Mr. Isch's store and to check on the tide table outside the front door of the little hotel, but mostly we ate the fish we caught off the rocks. Now and then we had a big feast of mussels steamed over seaweed on the rock hearth out toward the latrine.

The mussels and the fried-egg sandwiches are what I remember most thoroughly about those first years of learning to live well gastronomically, and I have already written too much about the sandwiches in other places. I should state clearly, though, that they must be made of good honest bread. The eggs should be about three or four days old, and if possible laid by hens with roosters nearby so that the yolks stand up properly. The bacon drippings must have attained that certain noble amalgam of all decent drippings added over several weeks to a clean old coffee can. And then the warm sandwiches must be wrapped not in plastic wrap but in waxed paper, the kind that will gradually begin to sweat and drip, so that by the time the sandwich is unwrapped, some of the paper sogs off on it and tastes fine, if you are hungry enough.

The only real attraction for this recipe for Fried Egg Sandwiches is harmless as well, since I am sure that Aunt Gwen is as strong a force in life as she ever was, and what is more, she is in everyone's life in one form or another. Her own ways of nourishing each one of us are less easy to put down than the recipe I remember for the fried-egg sandwiches. They are less identifiable, and therefore this one existent recipe may well serve us for all the other unidentifiable ways she and her kind continue to feed our bodies and souls.

I am glad the kitchen in Laguna has been razed or bulldozed. By now there may even be a condominium or high rise where it once leaned against our shack. Certainly the mighty trees are gone. But the Pacific still rolls and crashes against the rocks not two blocks westward, and probably fish still lurk nearby. And surely somewhere there is another little kitchen as impossibly ugly and inconvenient, where honest food waits for hungry happy children —a fish stew, or milk toast in a bowl . . . or a fried-egg sandwich.

—1983

5
The First Kitchen
(1912–1920)

It is impossible for me to think of the first kitchen in my memory without connecting it with my Grandfather Holbrook. This is odd because I don't remember him at all, although I think I met him once just before his death. I must have been very young, since I was almost four when Grandmother Holbrook, his widow, came to live with us.

The first kitchen was in the big house in Whittier where we lived from my third year until I was almost twelve, and I clearly remember thinking that it was the nastiest room I had ever seen in my life and wondering how my mother and father could stand to have good things come from it. They ate very well from there always, and I myself learned to cook in its dark green shadowy depths.

The kitchen was long, narrow, and dank, and it was the ugliest room in the house. It was lit by one electric bulb hanging from the center of the ceiling directly above the kitchen table, with its two bins for flour and sugar underneath and its chipped white enamel top. The only natural light came from two high windows above the kitchen sink at one end of the room, which I never was tall enough to look out of. There was probably a view of the house next door, but I don't remember ever seeing anything except a patch of sky far above the old sink.

The sink had a counter on either side, and it was very ugly, like everything else in the room. The stove was gas and it was against the far wall from the door into the dining room. There were many cupboards and one cooler and, of course, a small icebox. There was linoleum on the floor, and between the dining room and the kitchen, there was a small mysterious sliding door that was supposed to open onto a built-in sideboard in the dining room, but it was never used. The cook-of-the-moment brought everything in through the swinging door.

In the dining room, Mother had an electric bell under her foot that summoned the help from the kitchen, but she could seldom find it and instead would ring a little silver bell. Father sat at the kitchen end of the table and Mother at the far end so that she could keep one eye on the swinging door. I never knew how it was managed so smoothly, but the service was always good. We children never addressed the hired help during the meals, nor she any of us, although we might have been jabbering happily together just before entering the room.

At the sink and window end of the kitchen, which was painted greenish brown, a door led onto the porch, also long and narrow, where there was a small toilet and a tiny stuffy little room, with one window at its end, for the current slavey. The room was without ornament of any kind, and I suppose it had the usual bed and chair and even a bureau, and the woman who occupied it was supposed to use the back toilet and do all her other personal washing up in the kitchen sink. She was off every Thursday evening and Sunday after lunch and was considered part of the family, but always in a subservient way.

It seems odd now that I was raised with a strange woman always in the house, an imposition I never did like. My mother, who was born and raised on the plains of Iowa, considered such services as part of her life and always had someone to help with the daily chores or, in fact, to perform all of them. Most of her hired help had been Swedish and Norwegian people, immigrants learning the language, and in California she had to accustom herself to live with a much more motley group of people.

Our first maid-of-all-work was a very large black woman named Cynthia, who was without any pretensions or prejudices. She was there the first winter we were in Whittier, and she had the bedroom next to the bathroom upstairs. When Grandmother Holbrook came to live with us, the servant's room was added onto the back of the house, along with a little apartment for the autocratic old Irish lady.

Cynthia was wonderful, with warm skin, and my little sister Anne and I loved to crawl into bed with her and softly sing hymns and pray to her God. She sat proudly in the middle of the backseat of the Model-T Ford on Sundays when we went for our weekly drive, with Anne and me on either side of her and with Mother and father sitting grandly in the front seat, dressed in their dusters and Mother in a veil and driving hat. Cynthia seemed much grander—and we were especially admired by anyone who saw the spectacle—when she wore a high turban of blue satin with a matching dress that she inherited from Mother. The dress was cut very low with inserts of brown lace that did not show at all on her skin so that she looked like a half-naked goddess.

Cynthia soon left because she was the only black woman in

Whittier, and when she went to the grocery store for Mother, nobody spoke to her; nobody had seen her at all. "I am invisible here," she said. "I must go."

Mother and my little sister Anne and I wept, and even Father was much moved, although he admitted that he had always hated to go into the bathroom for his morning shave after Cynthia had steamed up the windows with her bath.

That was my first brush with racism, and the last bath ever taken by a servant in the house, as far as I know, and nobody ever seemed to mind, although as I grew older I wondered about such privacies.

After Cynthia left, my sister Anne and I grew to accept the fact that cooks lived downstairs in their own quarters. My father was amazed to learn early on that he and Mother were considered especially kind to their help. I was always puzzled by the difference in the cook's new quarters downstairs and our own bedrooms upstairs. There must have been some signs of the various occupants of that little room, but I don't remember any of them, not even a picture of a relative or a book or magazine. Anne and I freely used the back toilet, which made us feel close to the cook. We would spend long hours in that stuffy little cubbyhole, taking turns sitting on the toilet and listening to my continued stories, most of which concerned imaginary characters connected in some way with World War I.

I remember talking seriously with Mother several times about why the servant's room was so ugly, but she would tell me that she and Father were the best employers, and she also boasted to me that her own father had felt that domestic help should form a union. Grandfather Holbrook had even proposed it several times before his death, but he was always laughed at.

The kitchen remained dank and unappetizing, although it was most enjoyable when Mother would go down to make an annual cake for my father's birthday. (It was a Lady Baltimore cake, for some reason.) And there were times when Grandmother would supervise the making of jam there in the dark room, when once a year several cousins would appear bringing fruit from their ranches, and the kitchen would be full of laughter and good smells from the pots. Mostly, though, it was a place to avoid by everybody but me, except on Sunday nights when we would have supper to make by ourselves—very simple things like oyster stew or scrambled eggs.

I soon learned that the best way to get attention was to cook something, and I easily fell into the role of the cook's helper. I loved to stand on a little stool and stir things carefully in a double boiler, so that I soon became known as the family cook on the regular cook's night out. Early on I was helping her make cake on Saturday morning for Sunday noon.

After Cynthia came Amimoto.

It was late 1912, and everybody in southern California had a Japanese houseboy: there were thousands of them, learning English and engineering and diplomacy and such, going to school and living with American families who laughed in a more or less kindly way at them and told about their funny sayings at parties.

Amimoto was not unusual and did not, like many of his fellow refugees, later become an admiral or an ambassador or a suicide pilot. He was a gentle, polite, desperately homesick boy, and my mother was one of the worst people he could possibly have worked for because she was almost paralyzed by him, by his differentness from any male she had ever seen in her life: his different color and lack of beard, the way his eyes grew in his head, his soft way of speaking and moving, which to her seemed sinister because she may have seen someone like Sessue Hayakawa in moving pictures. Amimoto disturbed her to the point of hysteria, and although she managed to tell my father now and then of his more ludicrous mistakes in English or cookery, she was basically repelled and terrified by him the whole time he was with us. She was, always, an ideal person to work for, thoughtful and considerate, but if Amimoto knew that, he must also have known that she was not happy to be mistress to his servanthood.

I see now that the way he and my sister and I, on the other hand, were completely happy together must have worried her deeply. We understood one another without words, but I have been told what I do not remember, that he used to talk and sing to us for hours in his own language and that we understood that, too, as far as anyone could tell. And we had no trouble speaking our very simple English with him: we were not looking for mistakes in either his grammar or our own, nor were we conscious of amusement or curiosity but only of our real ease with him. He would take us for walks, up the hill past the little Quaker college he went to, or to the dusty City Park, or to the Children's Basement of the Library where he was slowly reading through a series called *What Katy Did: What Katy did at School, What Katy Did Abroad,* and so on. He read parts of these exciting stories to us, and later when I was old enough to devour them as he had done, from left to right along their shelf without a perceptible pause between volumes, I could still hear his delicate voice in my mind.

We used to lie on his bed (you can see how this would disturb my mother: she had been raised when *women* tended little children, especially little female children) in the hideous "maid's room" off the back porch, the three of us crosswise like stalks of asparagus, while he worked small pieces of whittled bamboo into puzzles. They were much too complicated for our small fingers, and I don't know what he did with them all—sold them perhaps or sent them home to his brothers and sisters. There was the stuffy dark cubbyhole next to his room with a toilet in it, and when we needed to go in there he would unbutton our panties deftly with one hand and keep on arranging the bits of bamboo with his other. Or if he was fixing vegetables for dinner, which he did every afternoon when he got back from school, he would scrub and pare and somehow go right on with his homework or his fascinating letters to Japan, written on soft paper that smelled much better than any we had ever seen. We would stand as close to him as we could, our heads just by his knees as he perched on the kitchen stool, and if Mother came in she would laugh self-consciously and shoo us out of the kitchen so as not to bother him. That was *her* story; ours was, of course, never mentioned, but the three of us understood that we could not possibly bother him, for he loved us and was lonely, and we loved him and were happier with him than with anyone else in the world, temporarily at least.

That fact, which must have been incomprehensible to my mother, was why he finally left, although the story always was about the way he fixed radishes one night. My mother was a sensitive and very intelligent woman, but in a thousand years she could never have recovered from her first basic uneasiness at him, at his smallness, his brownness, his softness. He simply was not human to her. What is more, it must surely have disturbed her to see that to us he was more than human, that he was divine.

The whole thing is logical. Mother hated him because we did not . . . and she got rid of him.

Once she was to have four guests for dinner, and there were special steamings and such-like in the kitchen, with brussels sprouts, a great delicacy in those days, sent out on the Pacific Electric from Jevne's in Los Angeles. Father brought them home at noon, and my sister and I watched Amimoto peel off their tiny outer leaves.

They were the right size for fairies. That is all I remember. The rest is apocryphal. It seems that when it was time for dinner to be served, there was none, and Mother found Amimoto hunched over the sink in the kitchen, carving radishes that had been meant as a garnish into exquisite little copies of the brussels sprouts and arranging the green and the rosy-white flowers in patterns on her best silver tray. Nothing had been cooked. Nothing had even been made ready. But the radishes and the raw vegetables were, even my mother had to admit, as beautiful as jade, as coral. . . .

That, the story went, was why Amimoto left: he was undependable.

My sister and I knew better, but we were powerless to do anything but grieve in secret. Now and then a long cylinder of thin rice cakes would come for us, and my mother would shake her head half-regretfully, half in amusement, over this continued sentimentality. She would tell about the radishes again, and we could not rightly enjoy the little cakes she said had come from Amimoto.

By the time I started to go to school, they had stopped coming, and people told us he had forgotten us, but I don't think so, for we never forgot him.

After Amimoto, the best help we ever had in the kitchen were four middle-aged sisters, the McClure girls. They lived with their father far down on Painter Avenue, and we never knew which of them would be serving breakfast. Bertha was tall and thin and very nervous, so that when she served coffee or tea the cups rattled in their saucers. We were aware that Bertha had a crush on Father and watched eagerly when she would slide around his unconscious head and titter helplessly when he addressed her directly.

Our favorite of the four sisters was Margaret, of course. She was almost as small as we were, a tiny woman with a cleft palate. My sister and I used to pray with her often in her bedroom and were unaware that for a long time we were speaking just as she spoke, as if we had cleft palates, too. Grandmother and Mother finally forbade Margaret to come to the house at all, as we always spoke just as she did when she was anywhere near us. This became, in fact, a real kind of fetish with my parents, especially my mother, and we had a hard time breaking ourselves of this habit. Margaret-talk became our secret language, and finally we had only to mutter the words *sixty-four* in her strange cleft palate accent to feel safe and loving, two united against the world. This continued until my sister died when I was fifty-seven and she was fifty-five, but it was a secret between us.

Margaret was the last of the four sisters to come, and I think I began to use the kitchen more as a show-off place after she left. By the time I was ten, I was thoroughly into cooking in that dreadful room, and I knew its worst secrets and knew equally well that there was no use in protesting its many discomforts. By then I could bake a fairly decent sponge cake and had learned not to experiment with changing the proportions of spices and such in recipes. I no longer needed to stand on a little stool to stir the white sauces and less commendable messes that catered to my grandmother's austere ideas of correct eating.

We left for the country when we moved down Painter Avenue across the county road and onto Painter Extension. The kitchen there was bright and cheerful, and the servant's quarters were separate from the house. By then, I realized that Mother and Father were indeed good employers, but I always wondered how they could have subjected other human beings to such sordid conditions as were taken for granted in the first big house on Painter.

I wished fervently that I had known my grandfather, and I still do, because he sowed the seeds in me of protest against conditions that were otherwise considered normal. He probably would have enjoyed the same good food, and he might never have voiced his critical views to the people most connected with these same views. He was most certainly not an agitator, any more than they were eager to be disturbed. In other words, it would all have continued in the usual patterns, but it is a comfort to me to know that my grandfather felt strongly about the conditions of servants in America. And I don't think that by now there are any slaveys, as we took for granted. Neither Grandfather nor I did anything to change the situation, but I feel sure that Cynthia would no longer be invisible, even in Whittier, and that anyone who had to live in that little room off the back porch would see to it that a bathroom was available somewhere in the house. But Grandfather would still be an unknown stranger to me, and I would still make white sauces for Grandmother and practice the powers that lurked behind my continued interest in cooking. In other words, the more things change, the more they are the same.

—1990

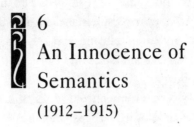

6
An Innocence of Semantics
(1912–1915)

Almost anyone who wants to can write by now of how pure the air was when he was a boy in Iowa, a child in the Bronx, how quiet the streets were, how fair the streams and gutters. Instead, most of us give a defeated shrug (or cough, or chest rattle). Yes, we have defiled our world. How could we know that it was happening? We frown with guilt and shrug again.

I can remember, though, that some forty-five years ago in Laguna Beach, clean rags and a bottle of kerosene began to be standard equipment for our all-day loiterings on the beaches, to clean our feet and our bodies of the black oil that floated down to us, several times a year, from the coastline fields. Sometimes the rims of the waves would be almost black with the stuff, and the beach would be fouled until we had a very high tide or a good storm. We shrugged in the Twenties, too: it was a small local problem—nasty, but what could one do?

By now the whales know better, and they have quickly

changed thousands of years of habit, and on their way to Mexico to breed, they avoid their ancient path between the Santa Barbara Islands and the mainland and stay far out from any possible oil slicks. Whales and seals and porpoises are smart, and so are sardines: they *git*.

Oysters, shrimps, trout, gulls, and pelicans—they have had a rougher time of it, perhaps, and already they are almost unknown in many of their old resting places and playgrounds. There is no livable water left for them. Perhaps their ways of communication are less advanced.

And for the air breathers, what is there?

My father worked with the first committees formed to study air pollution in southern California in about 1925. As a small-time citrus grower, he could already see what was threatening the orange and lemon groves; as a small-town editor, he could hear what some keen doctors were muttering: chest rattles in unborn babies, old men dying slowly from lack of oxygen in the streets. The second nearest I ever saw him to weeping in public was after a meeting one night in Monrovia or Glendora, made up of concerned people trying to talk with the unconcerned, the cupidinous. He was in a state of near-hysteria from frustration. There he was, a newspaper editor, by ethics a *voice*. But the big manufacturers, the oil refiners, the producers of patently noxious goods and gases would never hear him. They were deaf to everything the committee tried to tell them. He felt defeated, which is painful to the soul. He rose to fight again and often, of course, but from that night on there was a shrug, no matter how concealed, in his editorial stance.

Still, when we were first in Whittier, the air was good, and we used it as our rightful element, having been born in it. It blew gently to us and then up the mild slopes of the hills from the flatlands between Whittier and the sea, where some dairy cattle grazed and where there was cultivation of the less soggy ground:

potatoes, wheat. Then there was the ocean. Probably the air that reached us was blown for thousands of miles across waves and flowery islands. While I was a child, oil wells were sunk at Huntington Beach, but we never smelled them or thought of them in Whittier, and only occasionally did we in Laguna when the beaches were fouled and then washed clean again.

Many growing things cleansed the air for us and kept it sweet. The Spaniards and Mexicans had been great ones for planting, and olive trees flourished in long avenues and hilly groves around the town. There were fine stands of eucalyptus trees, which had been brought from Australia by adventurers who dreamed vainly of selling them to the government for telephone poles. They grew generously in the new land, and their seeds rolled here and there and took hold. The leaves sent out a steady subtle odor, almost dusty when the air was hot and still and as exciting as a new young wine when the trees were in bloom and the jade-gray horny buds produced their astonishing fragility of little honey-colored hairs.

Then the bees worked, high in the gangly trees and low on the ground, where sweet alyssum seemed to thrive in the soil that many gardeners felt had been forever contaminated by the oil in the eucalyptus leaves. (We had good honey in Whittier, before easterners came to demand nothing but that vapid syrup from the orange blossoms.) For twenty-five years of my life I listened to bees, high above me as I lay against a big fallen branch, and then watched them as they stopped, half-drunk, for a few sips of the tiny white weeds all about me. And when I was little my sister and I used to rub the tender new leaves roughly on our forearms and sniff ourselves: how clean and fine!

Another thing that made the air in Whittier special, to my inner nose anyway, were the great fields of wild mustard that almost surrounded us. It grew on the hills, of course. But between us and Los Angeles were long stretches of open meadows, and in the spring they were dazzling, like pale yellow gold. They sent up a wild sweet blast of perfume, an invitation almost, hinting of strange pleasures not yet understood. As we tooled sedately on a Sunday, in our open Model-T, toward Los Angeles or perhaps the Busch Gardens in Pasadena and got past Pio Pico's crumbling White House and over the Rio Hondo Bridge, the fields opened out on either side of us and rolled as far as we could see. There was the little village of Montebello, and from then on to the outskirts of Los Angeles, with its peculiar Chinese and Greek cemeteries, its huge brick Catholic orphanage, there was nothing but gold. On a still day, the air was so little moved by our cutting slowly through it that the honeyed heavy perfume almost drugged us.

And orange groves were being planted fast, to the south and east and even the hilly northwest of our town. Which was more profitable was the question: to raise the subtropical trees for their blossoms, to be shipped by canny Los Angeles florists to the eastern wedding markets, or to raise the fruit and risk having it freeze on the trees? Many people gambled on the second choice, like my father, and few of them made very much money, but they kept the air perfumed for us!

By the time I was nearing my teens, I felt that orange trees were the dullest bloblike growths on the planet, tidy and stupid in shape and crawling with several kinds of lice. I hated oranges because of years of surfeit and can still forgo them easily, except perhaps in a good marmalade or tart. But the word *ineffable* was made for the perfume an orange tree in full bloom will give forth, especially in the moonlight—and especially if it is near a lime or lemon, when the blend with oxygen is dizzying.

There were other things in Whittier to make our air better than almost any other I have breathed. Many of the old ladies, ancient widows or withered daughters of the First Settlers, cultivated bushes that had grown from the slips brought by Mrs. Aguilla Pickering and all her fellow Quaker ladies from their eastern and midwestern gardens; rose geraniums, lemon verbena, night-blooming jasmine grew everywhere around their houses.

The hills rose right above the town to the east and north, and they were still almost virgin, blanketed at the right times with poppies and blue lupine and a dozen other less obvious blossoms, all of them with their own subtleties of smell.

And there were no factories, few cars, and still plenty of animals, like horses and cows, to add their healthy blotters of good dung to the ecological balance.

The soil was young, as earth goes on the planet. It needed help, if it was going to be plowed and used. Cover crops were planted generously; it was found that the topsoil would not support the native weeds, once it had been turned over. When I first walked through a new orange orchard in what is now called La Puente, I was five or so, and poppies grew tall enough to brush my face and make the tiny fruit trees look foolish. Within a few years, though, the bright orange satiny blossoms grew only in roadside ditches, where their sensitive seeds could still take hold without risk, and ranchers planted controlled mixtures of weeds to add strength to the soil's minerals. They were murderous to walk through with bare legs, seeming to lean heavily on the nettle family.

By the time gases from the diesel trucks, the cars, and the factories started to stunt and kill the orange trees, all the fertilizers were prefabricated, so much simpler to spread, and anyway, where was there still for hire a worker who knew how to use a plow and disk? Then, for every tree that died, a new settler arrived and needed living space, and the oranges and lemons and walnuts were pulled out to make room for subdivisions, laid like cookies from a stucco pastry tube over the broken roots. By now there are no orchards, and most of the hills have been bulldozed and leveled into unrecognizable shapes, to offer dubious support for upper-bracket "ranch-type" or "Mediterranean" homes, and there are not any ditches left. They have been burned out with weed killers, as fire hazards, and the poppies are gone.

As for the water, I cannot imagine what the rivers are like now. When I was little, I knew the Rio Hondo best, because we crossed it often, and of course we used to get watercress from its upper banks.

Soon after we landed in Whittier, in 1912, there was a cloudburst and flood. The bridge between us and Los Angeles washed out and on down to the Pacific. My father, going against Mother's protests, took me out to the edge of what was left of the county road, and I sat in the back of the Ford while he photographed things like the pulley that had been rigged to get mail across the boiling yellow flood. A tree raced along in the middle of it, and in its bare branches a big gopher snake was looped intricately, its jaw set in a frantic impotent hiss as its strange craft whirled toward the sea.

I do not think that I would ever want to find out what has become of the little rivers that once ran down from the foothills of our part of southern California. They used to be laughed at by visitors from the East, who knew the Hudson and the Mississippi, for most of the time they were invisible or just little trickles into an occasional shallow pool. Their beds were wide and sandy, with willows always growing along them to make the air smell like witch hazel. There were three or four places where gypsies encamped. They were a dark and aloof people, up from Mexico to pick the walnut crops or to rest before another long move, but they never went near the Rio Hondo or any other "California river" in a season when a flash storm could stretch the banks in a few minutes with its crazy roar of racing water. I suspect that by now such potential danger has been piped underground to be used to carry effluent out to sea and that the wide white sands of the riverbeds have been paved for roads or covered with houses in straight lines.

My sister and I perfected one act of mimicry that at first amused Father and Mother in the front seat of the car, on our Sunday afternoon drives, and finally got on their nerves to the point where Mother said sharply, "Oh, please *stop* that!" and he said, "Yes, *do,* and *pronto.* Enough is enough." We understood that our vocal fun was over, but forever we would say silently, as we crossed the bridges in our home county, what for a short riotous season we had chanted in unison, in fluty shrill shrieks of exaggerated refinement, no doubt in mockery of some visiting relative: "Oh, *LOOK* at all the *PEEple, swimming* in the *RIvah!*" This would send us into whoops of delight and amusement every single time. What wit, we felt, what delicious sarcasm! There was no water in the river; there were no people to not-swim—oh, *hilarious!*

I can see how this proved boring to adults, but it lent a fine satirical sparkle to many a routine promenade for Anne and me. The backseat of a car driving slowly over familiar roads, Sunday after Sunday, can grow a little dull. . . .

Norman Mailer has written somewhere that the need of a city is to accelerate its growth, while the pride of the small town is to retard it. In California there can be no such pride, as thousands of people a month move across its blandly welcoming borders and elbow a place for themselves. Whittier's population is now over one hundred thousand. The soft hills have been cut into recklessly, to make holes and cliffs for houses, and native plants like poppies and lupine and holly and sage have been shaved away forever. Houses and stores sprawl clear to the continent's edge, half hidden by mustard-brown smog. Except for an occasional road sign, it is impossible to know when one has driven past the city limits of the "Queen of the Foothills," as the little Quaker settlement was called hopefully in its earlier days. When has one entered Montebello, if it still exists, or Norwalk or even Yorba Linda?

There used to be a good little co-operated orange packing-house on the edge of that last small settlement, and in another place nearer to us, La Habra, there was a weekly newspaper in a shabby little store building on the main street. After Father's own daily was safely off the presses, he would sometimes pile Anne and me into the car and take us spinning along the country road, through miles of orange orchards on the sloping land, past an occasional fine planting of walnuts. We would go into the big shadowy packinghouse, unless picking was in swing, when my sister and I would wait in the car. There was a bitter smell of discarded fruit, almost good to inhale, like medicine. Father would exchange views with anyone still hanging around the plant: Mexican pickers were much handier with the fruit than whites, but undependable; a new kind of smudge pot was being developed; young fellows from Whittier College should not be allowed on the nighttime crews of fumigators: they were too eager, and one whiff of that cyanide . . .

A little further back toward home, in La Habra, while Father went in to gab with his colleague, we sat in the car, decorously watching the housewives walk along the one sidewalk in the village, so different from our own comparative metropolis of almost five thousand people. Boys did tricks for us on their bicycles right on the main street, soft with dust. That would never have been permitted in Whittier, where Greenleaf and Philadelphia crossed to form the hub of business, traffic, *life*.

On the way home, toward the slanting sun, the orange trees looked taller, darker. As we turned up Painter, fine magnolias and sycamores and deodars that the first Quakers had planted sent great shadows across our street. It had been a nice jaunt, as always, in the lightly perfumed air. We were innocents, unaware of all the words that would someday change our minds. *Smog, pollution, effluence, ecology* itself were still part of an unsuspected semantics. We felt fine and hungry.

—1957

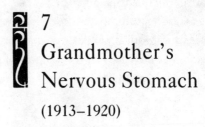

7
Grandmother's
Nervous Stomach
(1913–1920)

One of the fine feelings in this world is to have a long-held theory confirmed. It adds a smug glow to life in general.

When I was about five, I began to suspect that eating something good with good people is highly important. By the time I was ten I not only knew, for myself, that this theory was right but I had added to it the companion idea that if children are given a chance to practice it, they will stand an even better chance of being keen adults.

In my own case I was propelled somewhat precociously, perhaps, into such theorizing by what was always referred to in the family as Grandmother's Nervous Stomach, an ultimately fortunate condition that forced her to force us to eat tasteless white overcooked things like rice and steamed soda crackers in milk.

Now and then either Grandmother's stomach or her conscience drove her to a religious convention safely removed from us, and during her pious absences we indulged in a voluptuous riot of things like marshmallows in hot chocolate, thin pastry under the Tuesday hash, rare roast beef on Sunday instead of boiled hen. Mother ate all she wanted of cream of fresh mushroom soup; Father served a local wine, red-ink he called it, with the steak; we ate grilled sweetbreads and skewered kidneys with a daring dash of sherry on them. Best of all, we talked, laughed, sang, kissed, and in general exposed ourselves to a great many sensations forbidden when the matriarchal stomach rumbled among us. And I formed my own firm opinions of where gastronomy should and indeed must operate in any happy person's pattern.

A great many seemingly unrelated things can be blamed on a nervous stomach, as ladies of the middle and late years of Queen Victoria's reign well knew.

Here I am, for instance, at least ninety-five years after my maternal grandmother first abandoned herself to the relatively voluptuous fastings and lavages of a treatment for the fashionable disorder, blaming or crediting it for the fact that I have written several books about gastronomy, a subject that my ancestor would have saluted, if at all, with a refined but deep down belch of gastric protest. That I have gone further and dared link the pleasures of the table with our other basic hungers for love and shelter would outrage far more than the air around her, to be sure: kisses and comfort were suspect to such a pillar as she. They were part and parcel of the pagan connotations of "a cold bottle and a warm bird" or vice versa—wanton and therefore nonexistent.

The Nervous Stomach was to Grandmother and to her "sisters" in the art of being loyal wives and mothers of plump beardy men a heaven-sent escape.

The pattern was one they followed like the resolute ladies they were: a period of dogged reproduction, eight or twelve and occasionally sixteen offspring, so that at least half would survive the nineteenth-century hazards of colics and congestions; a period of complete instead of partial devotion to the church, usually represented in the Indian Territory where my grandmother lived by a series of gawky earnest missionaries who plainly needed fattening; and at last the blissful flight from all these domestic and extra-curricular demands into the sterile muted corridors of a spa. It did not matter if the place reeked discreetly of sulphur from the baths and singed bran from the diet trays: it was a haven and a reward.

In my own grandam's gradual but sure ascent to the throne of marital freedom, she bore nine children and raised several of her sisters', loaned from the comparative sophistication of Pittsburgh for a rough winter or two in what was to be Iowa. It is not reported by any of the native or transplanted youngsters that she gave them love, but she did her duty by them and saw that the Swedish and Irish cooks fed them well and that they fell on their knees at the right moments. She raised a good half of them to prosperous if somewhat precarious maturity.

As the children left the nest, she leaned more and more in one direction as her dutiful husband leaned in another, toward long rapt sessions with the Lord. Fortunately for the social life of a village such as she reigned in, His disciples were hungry, young, and at times even attractive, on their ways to China or Mbano-Mbang.

In a Christian way things hummed during the protracted visits of these earnest boys, and everyone lived high, even my grandfather who took to retreating more and more lengthily into his library with a bottle of port and a bowl of hickory nuts.

As inevitably as in the life cycle of a female mosquito, however, my grandmother passed through the stage of replenishing the vessels of the Lord, as she had already done through ministering to the carnal demands of her mate, and she turned to the care of her own spirit, as represented by her worn but still extremely vital body. She developed protective symptoms, as almost all women of her age and station did.

There were hushed conferences, and children were summoned from distant schools and colleges for a last faint word from her. She went on a "tour" with her husband to Ireland and the Lake Country, but for some reason it seemed to do him more good than it did her, and while he pranced off the ship in New York wearing a new Inverness cape, she left it retching and tottery.

At last she achieved what she had spent almost a lifetime practicing for, and she was sent *alone,* with no man or child to question her, to some great health resort like Battle Creek.

There the delicious routine laved her in its warm if sometimes nauseous security. Duties both connubial and maternal were shadows in her farthest heart, and even her morning prayers could be postponed if a nurse stood waiting with a bowl of strained rice water or a lavage tube.

One difference from our present substitute for this escape, the psychiatrist's low couch, is that today's refugees face few gastronomical challenges, unless perhaps the modish low-sodium-low-cholesterol diet can be counted as such. My grandmother found many such challenges in her years of flitting with her own spare crampish pleasure from one spa to another. Certainly what she could and would and did eat played a vigorous part in my own life, and most probably provided an excuse for my deciding to prove a few theories about the pleasures of the table in relation to certain other necessary functional expressions.

Grandmother did not believe in any form of seasoning, and in a period when all food was boiled for hours, whatever it was boiled in was thrown out as being either too rich (meats) or trashy (vegetables). We ate turnips and potatoes a lot, since Grandmother had lived in Iowa long before it became a state. We seldom ate cabbage: it did not agree with her, and small wonder, since it was always cooked according to her mid-Victorian recipes and would have made an elephant heave and hiccup. We ate carrots, always in a "white sauce" in little dishes by our plates, and as soon as my grandmother died I headed for the raw ones and chewed at them after school and even in the dark of night while I was growing. But the flatter a thing tasted, the better it was for you, Grandmother believed. And the better it was for you, she believed, the more you should suffer to eat it, thus proving your innate worth as a Christian, a martyr to the flesh but a courageous one.

All Christians were perforce martyrs to her, and therefore courageous, and therefore all good Christians who had been no matter how indirectly the result of Grandmother's union with Grandfather had to eat the way she learned to eat at such temples as Battle Creek.

They could eat her way, that is, or die. Several did die, and a few more simply resigned from the family, the way one does from a club, after the cook had served Grandmother's own version of white sauce once too often.

By the time she came to live with us—a custom most aging ladies followed then after their quiet withdrawn husbands, helped by gout and loneliness, had withdrawn quietly and completely— my sister and I had already been corrupted by the insidious experience of good cooking. Thanks to an occasional and very accidental stay in our big crowded house of a cook who actually cared whether the pastry was light or not, we had discovered the caloric pleasures of desserts. And thanks to an open house and heart to the south of us, where we could stay for dinner now and then while Mother was "resting," we had found that not all salad dressing need be "boiled" and not all fried things need be anathema. The mayonnaise: it was a dream, not a pallid loose something made of flour and oil and eggy water. The pineapple fritters dusted with white sugar: they were dreams, too, tiny hot sweet clouds snatched at by healthy children.

We soon learned, however, that to Grandmother's way of thinking, any nod to the flesh was a denial of her Christian duty, even to the point of putting a little butter on a soft-boiled egg, but although her own spirits as well as her guts may have benefited from the innocuous regime, ours did not.

Fortunately at least one of my grandmother's phases of development impinged upon another, so that when she felt herself hemmed in by ancestral demands, she would at one and the same time, in her late years, develop an extraordinary belch and discover that a conference was being held in a town at least thirty miles away, one in which there was a preponderance of well-heeled as well as devout dyspeptics. She would be gone a week or so, to anywhere from nearby Oceanside to a legendary religious beachhead somewhat south of Atlantic City. She picked conventions where she could drink a glass of lukewarm seawater morning and night for her innards, and it made slight difference to her whether the water was of Pacific or Atlantic vintage. It can never be known how coincidental were these secular accidents, but they were twice blessed for her and at least thrice for the rest of us: she could escape from children and grandchildren into a comfortable austere hotel, and we . . .

We? Ah! What freedom! What quiet unembarrassed silences, except for the chewings and munchings of a hundred things Grandmother would not eat!

No more rice water, opaque and unseasoned, in the guise of soup. No more boiled dressing in the guise of mayonnaise. No more of whatever it was that was pale and tasteless enough to please that autocratic digestive system.

She would start off, laced into her most rigid best, her Jane pinned firmly under the white spout of her noted pompadour. We would wave and smile, and as the Maxwell disappeared down past the college, with Father tall and dustered at the wheel, we would edge avidly toward the kitchen.

Mother would laugh only a little ashamedly, and then we'd make something like divinity fudge, a delicious memory from her boarding school days. Or if it was the cook's day off my sister would set the table crazily—ah, *la vie bohème*—with cut out magazine covers scattered over the cloth to make it crazier, and I would stand on a footstool to reach the gas burners and create.

Of course there were accidents, too revolting to detail here. But it was fine to feel the gaiety in our family, a kind of mischievous mirth, and at the same time all of us, even the small ones, sensed a real sadness that we could not share it with the short, stiff, dutiful old woman, eructating righteously over a dish of boiled carrots in a vegetarian cafeteria near her churchful of "sisters" and even "brothers."

It was magic always then to see the change in Father's and Mother's behavior at the table when Grandmother was gone. They were relaxed and easy, and they slumped in their chairs as the meal progressed. Mother would lean one elbow on the table and let her hand fall toward Father, and he would lean back in his chair and smile. And if by chance my sister or I said something, they both listened to us. In other words, we were a happy family, bathed in a rare warmth around the table.

It was then, I am sure, that I began to think of the spiritual communion of the act of peaceful eating—breaking bread. It is in every religion, including the unwritten ones of the animals, and in more ways than one, all of them basically solemn and ritual, it signifies much more than the mere nourishment of the body. When this act is most healthy, most healing to the soul, it obeys some of the basic laws: enemies do not break bread and eat salt together; one communes with others in *peace*.

And so we did, now and then when I was young. We met as if drawn together for a necessary communion as a family. The fact that we were refugees from the dietary strictures as well as the gastric rumblings of a spoiled stern matriarch added a feeling of adventure and amusement to those stolen little parties. We sipped and we dawdled, and I can still remember that occasionally we would *all* put our elbows on the table after dinner and Mother would sing, or she and Father would leave and let us stay on to indulge in the ultimate delight, in our pre-teen years, of putting a cupcake into our dessert bowls and covering it with sugar and cream. What ease, what peace, what voluptuous relaxation!

At home without Grandmother, we gobbled and laughed, and more and more I began to wonder about the meaning of happiness and why and how it seemed to be connected with the open enjoyment of even a badly prepared dish that could be tasted without censure of the tasting.

I was puzzled, of course, for I could not see why anything that made all of us so gay and contented could be forbidden by God. I did not know then, nor do I care to recognize now, the connection between self-appointed moral judging and the personal hair shirt of physical subjection, as my grandmother must have known it when she had to bear one more child and yet one more child because it was her Christian duty.

Now that I am much older, probably as old as she was when she first began to escape from her female lot by feeling dreadful pains throughout her Nervous Stomach, I can understand more of the why, but I still regret it. We escape differently now, of course, and today Grandmother would consult a couple of specialists, and perhaps stretch out on an analyst's couch, and then become a dynamic real estate broker or an airline executive or perhaps even a powerful churchwoman, which she was anyway. But she would have more fun doing it, of that I feel sure.

Of course, there was a slight element of sin, or at least of guilt, in the delightful meals we indulged in when Grandmother was not there, and as always, that added a little fillip to our enjoyment. I suppose my parents felt somewhat guilty to be doing things that Grandmother frowned on, like drinking wine or saying openly, "This is delicious!" My sister and I had not yet reached the age of remorse: we simply leaned back and sighed with bliss, like little fat kittens, unconscious of betrayal.

I think that I have been unfair to my grandmother. I realize now that what I've written about her has made many people think of her as hard and severe. She was neither. She was never a stranger in our house, and she taught me how to read and write, and I accepted her presence in my life as if she were a great protective tree. This went on until she died when I was twelve years old. I felt no sorrow for her leaving, but I missed her, and all my life I have felt some of her self-discipline and strength when I needed it.

Increasingly I saw, felt, understood the importance, especially between people who love and trust one another, of a full sharing of one of our three main hungers, which are for food, for love, and for shelter. We must satisfy them in order to survive as creatures. It is our duty, having been created.

So why not, I asked myself at what may have been a somewhat early age, why not *enjoy* it all? Since we must eat to live, why not make the best of it and see that it is a pleasure, something more than a mere routine necessity like breathing?

And if Grandmother had not been the small stout autocrat, forbidding the use of alcohol, spices, fats, tobacco, and the five senses in our household, I might never have discovered that I

myself could detail their uses to my own delight. If my grandmother had not been blessed with her Nervous Stomach, I might
never have realized that breaking bread together can be nourishing
to more than the body, that people who can sit down together in
peace and harmony will rise from the meal with renewed strength
for the struggle to survive. My grandmother, who was stern and
cold and disapproving of all earthly pleasure, because that was the
way she had been raised to think a Christian and a lady should be,
would never understand how she taught me otherwise. I revolted
against her interpretations of the way to live a good life, but I
honestly believe that I have come to understand as much as she of
the will of God, perhaps, as Saint Teresa said, "among the pots
and pipkins."

And like my grandmother, I am apparently touched with the
missionary zeal, the need to "spread the word"! At least, I *suppose*
that is why I began to write books about one of our three basic
hungers, to please and amuse and titillate people I liked, rather as
I used to invent new dishes to amuse my family. I had a feeling it
might make life gayer and more fun. A Nervous Stomach can be a
fine thing in a family tree, in its own way and at least twice removed.

—1971

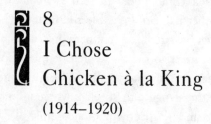

8
I Chose
Chicken à la King
(1914–1920)

Everyone, no matter how much he likes the life he is leading, has an escape hatch. Often he is unaware of it as such. More often he recognizes it, or even invents it, to save his inner balance, commonly called his reason.

My parents, living in a pattern circumscribed and dictated by their backgrounds and their ambitions, occasionally fled Whittier in a vaguely nervous way, as if a dog were nipping at their heels. Inside the invisible walls of our good Quaker compound, there was of course no alcohol, just as there was no riotous living. People who believed in "plain living and high thinking" ate simple food in their own quiet homes, and two or three dismal cafés took care of transients, except for respectable drummers who could put up at—and with—the Pickering Hotel. My father had to stay there when he was dickering for the *News*. It was grim, I understand, at least in its provender. It was not a place where a man would want to take his lady for a gastronomical frolic.

So Rex and Edith Kennedy would take off in the Ford now and then for "dinner in town." That meant Marcel's, I think, and the Victor Hugo, and a couple of other places either downtown in Los Angeles or on the sportier outskirts. Occasionally Mother brought us back a tissue paper hat or a rolled whistle that would shoot out when blown, with a pink feather at the end perhaps. We would discuss the menu at length, slowly and sensually. By the time I was six, I knew several names of procurable California wines, and I can remember Cresta Blanca for its beautiful sound, although I have never tasted this brand. (Only a few years ago, when we dug out part of the abandoned cellar of the house I now live in, a half-bottle with the Cresta Blanca label on it rolled to the top of the rubble, and I brushed it off respectfully and then gave it to a collection of local artifacts.)

When my parents went to the Scarlet Dens then available and pleasing to them, they ate and drank as they could not do at home—things like mushrooms under glass bells and sometimes two wines, matter-of-factly, not the one bottle sipped occasionally for a family festival. A white wine and then a red! It sounded almost too beautiful, as did the way things were served by the waiters to each person, instead of being put in front of Father and then carried around by Bertha or Margaret or whoever was holding down the kitchen at the moment. Through my mother's long happy descriptions of her rare sorties, I grew to feel almost familiar with *la vie mondaine* as she lived it, and when the time came for me to visit my first restaurant, I was ready.

I was about six, I think. The D'Oyly Carte troupe was playing at the Mason Opera House. I am sure there was a lot of planning done, with overt disapproval from Grandmother for such extravagant tomfoolery, unfitting to our years, and it was decided that Mother and Anne and I would take the Electric to Los Angeles, have lunch at the Victor Hugo, and then go to the matinée of *H.M.S. Pinafore* and take the Electric home.

It is a wonder that I did not break my string like a balloon and float off before the day, so excited was I. I am glad I did not, for the restaurant was exactly as I had known it would be: white tablecloths gleamed more brightly than ever at home, and the silver twinkled more opulently, if without our Irish hallmark, and on each little table in the hushed room were several roses in a tall vase that made my little sister and me look up at them somewhat as we did to the star on the Christmas trees that had so far dignified our only debauchery. And kind waiters pulled out our chairs, which had already been discreetly heightened for us, although I do not know how: perhaps a couple of middle-sized baking pans covered with towels? Napkins were whisked open in the air, like stiff clouds, and then laid across our especially scrubbed knees. Mother was given a menu.

It was then that I tried my first deliberate step into the sea of public gastronomy. I asked firmly a question I had been practicing for a couple of days. It was based on everything I had learned from Mother's recountings of her flights from the family board. I said, "May we eat chicken à la king?"

It is quite possible that this caused a little ripple of interest if not hilarity among the staff, but all I remember is that we seemed to have a covey of black-coated men bending attentively over us for the next two hours, cutting all kinds of capers with the enormous silver chafing dish, the large glittering spoons, the general air of excited well-being. Mother probably sat back happily and watched the game. I took double enjoyment from seeing and tasting a dish she had often described to me as one of her favorite things in the whole world (I doubt this . . .). Anne very probably started, that noontime, her lifelong inability to do more than nibble at food in public places: forever she would ask for something special and then seem to sneer at it or push it away, so that it became family legend that her eyes were bigger than her stomach, or something like that. As I recall it now, I ate heartily, observed everything, and had enormous fun. The flame burning under the dish interested me. The hot plates interested me, and the simple but subtle flavors. The waiters interested me.

When we had to leave, after some kind of dessert I cannot remember, my sister folded her napkin with unusual nicety and then asked the headwaiter, "Do these poor men have to wash all those dishes? May we help?" We swept out on this tag line, and as always, she had timed it perfectly to win every heart.

The rest of the day went well. I still remember Buttercup, who was indeed very plump and jolly. The best part was during the intermission, when Mother let me stand up on my seat to watch some of the audience go outside, and a tall Hindu wearing a large pale turban and a silky beard walked past our row. *"Jesus,"* I cried out excitedly to my parent and the rest of the theater. "Look! It's Jesus, all right!" This should have pleased my grandmother: one Christian impulse in an otherwise pagan fiesta. I am not sure that it did. My thoughts dwelt on other possibilities. I had tasted "sin and iniquity," and I wondered with impatience when I would next be able to eat chicken à la king with a flame under it, and perhaps someday much later order one or two wines to twinkle and shine on the impeccable linen of a Scarlet Den.

As far as I can remember, we kept our orgies well removed from Whittier during my childhood and forever beyond it. Except for almost secret temples like the Elks Club and the Parish House for seasonal routs, and our own home for quiet little gastronomical celebrations when Grandmother was away and we could indulge in such foreign stuff as French dressing, there seemed nowhere to go in the town.

And Prohibition cut heavily through the lists of good places farther afield.

As local editor, Father was wise enough not to be seen drinking in some of the dimly lighted ex-French restaurants in the region, although he continued to leave the sherry and port decanters on the sideboard and buy pinch-bottle Scotch from runners stationed off San Pedro. Marcel's was hard hit, and I think it closed, after a shady decline as an "inn," which in those drab days was synonymous with "roadhouse" and therefore with "speakeasy." A place I never went to until I was in my forties, the Goodfellows Grotto, managed somehow to stay open and relatively unshattered, thanks largely to its loyal newspapermen and lawyers. The Victor Hugo, which I believe used to be down on Spring Street, moved uptown to Olive between Fifth and Sixth or something like that, and in a mysterious and obviously well-backed way it stayed elegant throughout the dismaying cultural crisis brought on the nation by doughty ladies like my grandmother, who had fled alcoholic Northern Ireland only to land in the sodden Saturday nights of the midwestern prairie villages.

The "new" Victor Hugo was upstairs—shades of the Elks Club! The carpeting was soft and thick. Of course the linen and the mock silver gleamed and twinkled. The waiters, some of whom remembered us, or at least my little sister and her ladylike concern for them, seemed to scud along on invisible roller skates to whisk things before our noses. There was, within my memory, a lengthy prix fixe dinner that began God knows how but ended with a Nesselrode pudding, and my mother would always say faintly, "Oh, no," as I firmly settled for it, while she and Rex sipped cognac from their demitasses, in proper Prohibition style.

Once when we ate something under glass bells, one bell sealed itself hermetically to the plate, under which braised sweetbreads slowly died in their artful sauce, and the waiters puffed and groaned, and finally my father suggested that we continue with our meal and that a double-grilled lamb chop be brought to him, *rare*. Another time I went to luncheon with a contingent from home. I do not remember any of them, because Miss Hope was there, and in my heart and eyes she was the most beautiful fairy princess of them all, a tall slender woman with a soft rich voice and enormous eyes, perhaps gray.

The noon buffet of salads and hot things over flames was always exciting to me, but that day I ate shrimps in honor of my lady.

We never ate shrimps at home. Most probably it had not occurred to Mother to see if she could even buy any. In Iowa they were undoubtedly alive in the good fishing streams, but if anyone ate them it was the Indians. (Only a few hours ago, when Mr. Villa the fish man blew his horn along the street for us St. Helena ladies, I got some tiny defrosted bay shrimp from him for a Solari salad, and the elderly neighbor from across the street watched me with strange coyness and then squealed a little as she said, "Oo, I've always wondered about those things! Of course, I'm from Wisconsin." I told her they were delicious but that of course she had millions of them in the streams at home, the freshwater kind. She looked as shocked as if I had proposed eating a slice of her grandmother, and said, "Oh, we never eat anything but trout from our brooks in Wisconsin." Mr. Villa and I smiled invisibly at each other.) I had never, heretofore, put a succulent shrimp in my mouth, fresh or tinned. They looked in a distant way rather like curled snails, and I did not like anything that slid silently along, in water or on dry land. But Miss Hope was there, and in a gesture of which I am sure she was quite unconscious, I served myself generously from the great pile of them in the silver bowl, let the waiter help me add mayonnaise, and walked to our table in front of the tall open French window.

Below us the gentle sound of Los Angeles traffic circa 1920 purred past. Somewhere nearby Miss Hope sat, speaking melodiously to the other older people at our table, her great eyes haunted and her long nose twitching in a way that later seemed quite familiar to me when I fell in love aesthetically with Virginia Woolf. The first shrimp was a test of courage and honor for me, because of my conditional aversion to its general shape, but once I tackled it my whole life changed, and I knew that I would never feel anything but pure enjoyment again on contemplating in any and all forms the subtle water beast, the scavenger. No ugly tale could turn me from enjoying it, nor ever has.

I like to think that Miss Hope missed sipping a glass of good white wine with her lunch that magical day. I know that she was used to a less austere life than we all led in those strange times of the national disrepute of an age-old panacea. In Whittier I am sure she drank an occasional glass of wine with her family, the Lewises, when they all lived in our old house on Painter, and I know they drank a little sherry or whiskey at the Ranch. But that day in the twinkling sunlight at the Victor Hugo, when I really broke through a possible dietetic prejudice in order to prove my love, should have been graced with an important vintage. And perhaps it was.

—1971

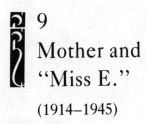

9

Mother and
"Miss E."

(1914–1945)

Edith, my mother, really understood dried-up hometown librarians better than anyone I know. She had a pet one always on hand when we were in Whittier and was in cahoots with her about things like my bringing home eight books once, when I was perhaps six, from the children's basement in the public library. The young (but already dried-up) librarian, of course, called Mother and told her that I had lied through my teeth, since I knew that only two books were allowed to be taken out at night by children. Mother was properly chilly and embarrassed.

Then the young dried-up librarian said she wondered how old Mrs. Holbrook was getting along. My mother replied that her mother was doing very well indeed and had not been ill for some thirty years, and then it came out that I had told the librarian my poor old Irish grandmother was on her deathbed and that she needed me to read to her . . . all night long, every night. Of course, this blatant fantasy was nipped in the bud, and from then on I was allowed to take only four books out at night, instead of the usual two.

As I look back on it, the episode proved Edith's power over the whole system, and I am glad that I was to benefit from it all my life, or at least until after she died. It was then that I realized *why* (and *when* and *how*) Mother had always been, in her bizarre treatment of dried-up librarians. I learned at last that Miss E., who for some twenty years had been the object of our extreme disaffection as well as mockery, had loved Mother dearly and loyally. This was partly because once a year, at Christmas, Edith always sent her a flamboyantly sexy and extravagant nightgown.

Of course, as we matured, we knew of these strange gifts, and Mother herself even discussed them and now and then showed us her yearly purchases with what was almost a titter from her and a universal snicker from us, her children. She'd spread out the beautiful gauzy flimsy whimsies over her bed, and we would make cruel, stupid, and often funny remarks about them, and about the person whose skinny old body they would soon hang on.

Of course, we envied Miss E., or her temporary equivalents, for we were young and spoiled and at times even given to moments of beauty, and Mother never bothered to shower us, her offspring, with any such extravagant dainties. This was a yearly custom, one of many in our household, but one we all puzzled over with obviously latent jealousy. We were convinced that Miss E. never really knew what to do with these exotic offerings.

Then, after Edith died, the dried-up librarian wrote to me from her desert "retirement home" such loving and even adoring letters as I hoped never to see again. They were amazing to me, and I knew that Edith had been right and that she had not bought the servitude of the strange remote disagreeable "old maids" for all those years in Whittier but that she had instead understood and appreciated something that was beyond our own caring or understanding.

To us, the children, Miss E. was a kind of ridiculous public dictator of our tastes and needs. We hated her for refusing ever to give us anything from the Closed Shelves, even when Mother would telephone to request that these sacrosanct supplies of local pornography and filth be opened to us. Miss E. stayed adamant, even in the face of Mother's yearly Christmas sensuality; she refused to heed the doctors, the local priests, and the pastors when they suggested that some troubled soul might find in her library a book that would instruct them better than their professional ethics could.

Once, when I came home from boarding school in a real puzzlement about the lesbian pleasures that were suddenly too much for me to understand and Mother asked Miss E. to let me take some books from the Closed Shelves, there was a firm *no!* Briberies, Christmas or otherwise, apparently meant nothing to this strange arbiter of our local morals. Mother ordered copies of most of Freud, Jung, Adler, and Krafft-Ebing, carefully and through "our" doctor Horace Wilson, and after she and I read them, she presented them to the library, as she had almost all the other good-dirty-sad books that were on the Closed Shelves there.

I remember that while we were waiting for the currently undesirable psychological exposés to arrive, Mother saw to it that I read *The Well of Loneliness* by Radclyffe Hall before she presented it to the Closed Shelves. Miss E. never acknowledged the presence of any of these books, just as she never thanked Mother with anything but a short impersonal note at Christmastime for her sexy nightwear.

Edith was Miss E.'s despair in many ways. She asked for and got any book that she did not care to invest in herself, and her deplorable taste in detective stories was locally known by anyone who visited the library, since Miss E. religiously let her read them first, before they went on the public shelves. Thanks to Mother's cryptic and avid habits, we had complete runs of every English writer of mysteries, from Agatha Christie on up and down, and our collections of Dorothy Sayers and her ilk were the best and the newest always, in California or even in America. Of course, our own shelves were always full of new books as well as old ones, but Mother was not about to invest in everyday literature when Miss E. was so amenable to her suggestions, and I feel sure that the Whittier Public Library circulated more current British and even American fiction than any other small Carnegie in the country.

Of course, Mother loved anything *English,* but her taste was good. We read *The Forsyte Saga,* but we also knew all about Vanessa Bell and the Bloomsbury gang almost as soon as they did themselves, and Leonard Woolf and his wife were as familiar to us as were the Churchills and even their American counterparts, the Roosevelts of both Republican and Democratic leanings. The Hogarth Press worked hard to provide us with Anglophilic trash as well as the "good" stuff. We read *The Spectator,* along with the *Times* and the lesser London kitsch, and all the American periodicals that were then in the mails.

This last important part of our literary upbringing was due less to Edith than to my father Rex, who subscribed to every periodical in print in America, whether or not it was free to him. He himself read probably ten magazines a week, and we all had a running undeclared war with him about remembering the plots of each continued story in every one of them. We prided ourselves on never reading the weekly résumés, and it was a game that was played with great success for more years than I can now remember.

Father, of course, read the magazines first, but as soon as he laid down an issue, it would be snatched up by one of us children and read as fast as possible.

Colliers and *The Saturday Evening Post* had perhaps the best serials, but there were also real dillies in magazines like *The Ladies' Home Journal* and *The Woman's Home Companion* and *Redbook* and *Cosmopolitan.* And then of course there was *The American Boy.* And Grandmother Holbrook saw to it that we always got— and *read*—*The Youth's Companion.*

And then there were all the magazines like *Motion Picture,* and there was something about automobiles always, and there were several farm journals and then house organs of clubs and organizations: Elks, 4-H'ers, and later Rotarians and Lions and the Kiwanis Club, and *The Iowa Morticians' Quarterly.* And then there were the literary digests—*The Atlantic Monthly* and *Scribner's,* wonderful things by Aldous Huxley about LSD or mescal buttons, and a long story by Scott Fitzgerald once, and always Upton Sinclair somewhere around—and Bernarr Macfadden's several different monthlies, all about diet and physical culture and how to conceive boy babies instead of girls, and so on. And there was *The Masses,* which I read hungrily when I was thirteen or so.

And all the time, as a kind of background to Mother's Anglomania and Father's Chicago-to-Whittier newspaper life, there were the reminders of Miss E.'s disapproval of our concerted and wild-eyed literary spree, which continued uninterrupted from about my fourth year in Whittier to the final bulldozing of the Ranch house when I was nearing fifty. By now I think of Miss E. as a sort of goddess, unwitting certainly and willy-nilly, floating austerely above our unconscious heads, wearing a very sexy nightgown over her presumably chaste body. She's rather like the airborne fellow who plays the fiddle in many of Marc Chagall's pictures: omnipresent and unexplained. She's much clearer now than when she was trying so desperately to curb our hungers and to keep them under proper local control.

In actuality, she was a tall, thin woman with faded colorless hair and skin, and she dressed properly in clothes that would fit her position as head librarian, which is to say in a way that made her almost invisible. At least, that is how I remember her in the name of my grandmother and my parents and my siblings. But by now, and in my mind anyway, and from her letters to me when my mother died, she has turned into a really loving woman, gracious and adoring, dressed always in those sheer, alluring, glamorous, and completely unfitting nightgowns that my mother gave her for so many years, in spite of our derisive mockery. And I wonder who actually got the most pleasure from them. Certainly my mother did not need to buy her way through the Closed Shelves, any more than Miss E. needed to be so unfailingly severe and disapproving.

—*1988*

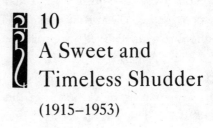

10
A Sweet and
Timeless Shudder
(1915–1953)

This is a footnote on either the general study of gastronomical atavism or on the disappearing profession of candy selling in front of movie houses and theaters. As far as I know, the old white-dressed men with trays of nougat and suchlike hung over their shoulders are gone, at least from downtown Los Angeles. But I know, too, that when I watched my two girls on the Quai des Belges in the old port of Marseille eat some of the same powdery candy that I first ate from one of those trays, it put me back to when I was six or seven.

The memory came to me as I was doling out some incredibly sticky powdery little slabs of what is called something-or-other Loukhoum in Marseille and what was called Turkish Delight in Los Angeles in 1915 and may still be: my two children shuddered and puffed with pleasure over its inimitable sweetness. Ah, they sighed, blowing out little gusts of powder. Oh, how good.

And poignantly I remembered doing that so long ago, when

my mother got three press passes and boarded my sister Anne and me onto the Red Electric into Los Angeles on a Saturday afternoon to the Orpheum Theatre, on Broadway, I believe. All I can recall of the first of perhaps a hundred such performances in the next ten years are some trained white dogs and then the way the big numbers changed at each side of the stage for the next act of vaudeville. There was an orchestra. (Other times there was Nora Bayes, a music hall singer, loud and tricky, whom my father considered worth driving in for, in the Maxwell or the Hupmobile or whatever he was driving or could borrow, when she played within driving distance.)

Inside the Orpheum, all was pulsating excitement and the throb of drums to such young ears as ours, so uncalloused by the artful assaults of radio and TV. Outside, there was the still-timid tinny sound of what was beginning to be called traffic. A great many rich easterners were flocking to neighboring towns such as Pasadena, and while the electrics driven by their wives never got as far into Los Angeles as the Orpheum, the gentlemen and even their offspring occasionally ventured there in high black-and-tan motorcars with basketwork on the outside of the doors and American Beauty roses nodding in crystal bud vases inside.

There were, of course, a few grim-jawed Bohemians like my father who got their wives into veils and dusters and their children under wraps and set out a good hour before curtain time in their open cabriolets, and on nights when they could get away without the kids they stopped usually at Marcel's for a good French dinner, wine included. All this giddy brouhaha of street sounds went on then, but the thing outside the Orpheum for my sister Anne and me was the candy man.

He was very dignified and withdrawn, with thick white eyebrows and a white mustache and small hands in thick white cotton gloves behind a kind of glass bulge over the tray on his stomach, a transparent screen that would seem normal to modern children accustomed to such things but to us was immeasurably mysterious, unaccustomed as we were to the fact that rubber and even glass could be made to curve that way and be seen through.

He had a little hammer, which he tapped remotely on pieces of marble, as white as his hair and hands. Our mother said it was nougat. This meant nothing to us, and I had to go to France years later to find out what nougat was—probably because many of Mother's teeth were not very strong at her age and she was afraid to buy a bag of it.

Then deeper on the tray, in a kind of mud or dust or embedment of confectioners' sugar, were oblong pieces of Turkish Delight. Ah, thank God my mother's teeth could handle that! She bought some the first day we ever went to the Orpheum.

We sat in a kind of trance with the orchestra of real-live people pounding on drums for the clown's pratfalls and sawing on violins for the love duet, and the clever little fluffy dogs, and perhaps even Nora Bayes, and as we watched we reached happily, blindly, for the candy, so that by the time we came out, still happy and even blinder, into the bright bald Los Angeles sunlight, we were covered from chin to hem and up both navy-blue serge arms with powdered sugar.

Mother flapped maternally at us as we staggered toward the Pacific Electric Depot, and we managed to get clear back to Whittier, some fourteen miles away, without feeling motion sick. It was a triumph of music over mind, perhaps, or the mystery of that old man with the transparent bubble on his belly and his little white hands inside it, doling out the powdery candy, the hard stuff and the insidious sweet Delight.

We often bought more from him, after that first day, and many years later I would go by and feel guilty about not stopping to see him, smaller but always white and dignified, beside the empty, dirty, near-deserted old theater. I could still taste the voluptuous stickiness of that candy, and then when my two girls shuddered happily at it on the Quai in Marseille, I was back in the Orpheum in Los Angeles, with its black velvet curtain covered with diamonds, the curtain that parted after the fire curtain with its wonderful paid advertisements was raised, while the men in the orchestra pit threw themselves wearily into the West Coast eleven-man version of Wagner's *Overture to Tannhäuser.* That curtain, that music, that two-hour dribble of powdered sugar! Is it a kind of atavism that made my children shudder the same way, so many years later, at the same gummy taste and texture of a candy? Or is it only my own memory that made me want to think they did?

—*1957*

11
The Old Woman
(1915–1916)

When I was halfway through the first grade, the private kindergarten that met every day in the Sunday school rooms of the Friends' Church went the way of most such ventures in a small and democratic town, and Anne came to Penn Street School.

I felt aged and responsible. For a while I held her little fat hand all the way from our house to the door of the girls' basement, which had been painted white and yellow and decorated with paper animals to make it look more like a kindergarten than a barren toilet.

As soon as she knew the way, she was impatient to be independent of my rather oppressive guardianship. But I made her walk close beside me when we crossed the two deserted streets between our house and school, and on the playground I sometimes quelled her into taking my hand.

There I liked to have the other girls see me leading her. I was the only one in the first grade who had a younger sister in Penn, and I felt that I should make the most of it.

How I should have hated to be my classmate Evelyn Wolf, who came every morning and afternoon in the tow of her big sister Emma, who was in the third grade! If Emma had been in the fourth, which was the highest in the school, there would have been something almost envious about being seen near her or even touching her, but in our minds the third was much less awesome. In the fourth you learned Long Division, whatever that was. Sometimes we heard the girls talking about it, and it sounded magical, like Aunt Gwen's songs from New Zealand.

But Emma Wolf was without much distinction, and poor Evelyn was uninteresting. Perhaps Evelyn felt the disgrace of being led around by such a plain thing.

I knew that Anne felt differently. She thought I was much older than an ordinary first-grader, if she thought at all. That was almost enough. And of course I had nice hair, not two little dust-covered twigs with dirty pink ribbons braided into them, like the Wolfs'.

I would make her hold my hand as long as I could. And I knew that if anything went wrong, she would take it instinctively. I almost hoped for trouble—not real trouble, but something that would be easy for me and hard for my sister.

On the way to school, I liked to walk past the house with the high fence around it, because sometimes a dog came bouncing toward us. He was small, and the fence was high. But his bark sounded vast, and Anne's hand always clutched mine desperately.

If I hadn't had her there to impress and show my bravery, I would have been half a block down the street before the end of the first bark, or perhaps I wouldn't even have walked on that side of the street at all.

With her there, though, I went slowly, holding her hand

firmly and sneering toward the furious little dog. It was a great moment, and one that seemed never to fail me.

Other things were less certain. There was a visiting dog, once, in a house farther up the street. He gave me a bad moment, which was all the more delicious for its first terror when I had made sure that he was on a chain.

And sometimes automobiles appeared unexpectedly far down the streets as we crossed them. Then I would seize Anne's hand and run madly for the opposite side of the curb, a full five minutes before it was necessary. But that happened rarely on the quiet streets of Whittier, so long ago.

By Eastertime my moments of lordly protection had narrowed down to the little dog, and even that was wearing away. I noticed that his most horrible barks had less and less effect on my sister. My power was slipping.

On the school grounds interest in the new little fat girl had died away, and it was more trouble than it was worth to make Anne take my hand and keep it to the door of the kindergarten room. And now the dog, too, was becoming almost friendly, and her fear of him less real.

It was then that I invented the Old Woman Without a Face.

She lived in a dark green house on the corner opposite the little dog's place, the one with the blinds always down. We had never noticed it before, Anne said. That was true, but only because I didn't want to scare her. Now, though, I must tell her: the Old Woman Without a Face lived in it!

She was a witch of the most terrible sort—no face, no children, no furniture. She lived on grass, which she crept out to pick at midnight, and on old shoes stolen at the same horrid hour from rag bins.

She was little, with long black hands.

But the worst part was her face, because it wasn't a face at all.

What was it? Just—a place. Yes, just a place where a face should be.

My poor little sister turned gray with fright and cowered beside me. I looked at the terrible blank green house. I, too, was scared. What if the Old Woman Without a Face should—Horror!

I grabbed Anne's clammy fingers and we ran for our lives, clear to Penn Street School and the welcoming busyness of the playground.

And for the rest of that year and even into part of the next one, I was the firm protectress of my sister Anne. We grew to know almost the whole history of the Old Woman, but I always stopped talking about her when I felt my flesh begin to crawl with terror. It took just a small dose to restore any of Anne's waning need for my presence.

The Old Woman was a dreadful creature, but when I wasn't near her dark green house, I almost liked her.

—1957

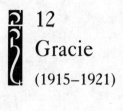

12
Gracie
(1915–1921)

I

It was a sunny day, with soft warm air in all the cracks. I could feel the softness and the warmth between the back of my neck and my hair where it hung in heavy pieces, and in my ears air seemed to move with a new freshness.

The windows of the schoolroom were open even during classes. Usually Miss Newby put them down at the end of recess or at most left them open three inches from the top, like the picture in the third-grade hygiene book. But today was different.

It was almost spring, Mother had said. If this weather kept up, Anne and I could change into cotton underwear!

Anne was so little she had forgotten the wonder of that annual shedding of woolen shirt and panties, but I remembered two times when I had taken them off before an afternoon bath and felt almost naked in the thin cotton things I had put on afterwards in place of them.

Today was Thursday. If tomorrow was like this, perhaps we could change on Saturday.

I snapped the rubber that held up my panties and looked out the windows. The first-grade room didn't have curtains. It was because we were too little, maybe. But we made flowers and birds and pointed green trees at Christmastime, and Miss Newby put them on the glass while we were home. Then in the morning we would see them as a surprise, sharp against the sharp clearness of the windowpanes and not at all as if they were meant to be there.

This month we had a row of red and yellow tulips springing starkly from the brown wood of the frames. It was pretty, I thought, when the windows were closed. But now it made me smile: paper tulips looked better close to the floor and not stretched tightly across the air up near the top of the room.

Gracie Meller, across the aisle from me, saw me peering at them and glanced up quickly, too.

She hoped to see something exciting. It was Gracie who always told us about accidents and houses that burned down and babies that fell into laundry tubs. She seemed to be everywhere just at the fatal moment and had a fine memory for details, especially ones of gore and shriekings and the crack of bones. But this time she saw nothing much.

She looked loweringly at me from under her thick black Mexican eyebrows. I watched her expectantly, my ludicrous tulips forgotten.

She moved her jaws deliberately, her eyes fixed on mine and daring me to look away. Then she slowly pursed her wide mouth into a tiny purple knot like the middle of a starfish.

It trembled. I watched it, without breathing. It seemed hours, but I knew Gracie would finish things somehow. It would be worth waiting for.

The purple knot settled into a firmer pucker. And suddenly a bright green worm shot out from the middle of that place. My mouth fell open. Back darted the worm. Gracie looked impassively at me, so I knew it wasn't over.

The next time the worm came out a little farther. It was clear and shining and not very long, and it seemed to have no head. I leaned closer to see it. It darted back, with a little pop as if it had closed the door after it. Gracie winked at me.

I sat motionless. I was glad my hair was getting long, because when I bent my head that way I couldn't see Miss Newby. And of course that made it impossible for her to see me.

I watched Gracie reach slowly into her desk. For another worm? Was it loose in there? I hoped not; it might fall into the aisle and be stepped on. That would be nasty, certainly.

Gracie worked at snail speed, as if she were opening a secret door. Her hand hardly moved, and I envied her skill but wished she would be less mysterious.

Miss Newby was writing at the big desk in the front of the room. I could hear her pen swerving steadily across the paper. There was no danger, but Gracie worked her fat brown hand into the desk with infinite caution. I began to feel very excited, like Jack in the sleeping giant's room.

The hand came slowly out of the desk, holding a small sack of gray paper with faint lines of blue and red on it.

The corner store! Gracie must have stolen some more money. Gracie was a bad girl, I thought. Mother had said so. But I liked her because she was so surprising and so courageously rude to people I had to be polite to.

She opened the sack neatly with one hand. The paper was soft and hardly made a sound. But Miss Newby stopped writing. I kept my head down, and Gracie's shiny black eyes shifted quickly from my face to her primer.

I felt a hideous need to giggle or sneeze or call out. But it would be a pity to miss the secret of the bright green worm. I thought as hard as I could about the paper bag still held lightly in Gracie's hot hand, and her purple mouth, and the way the worm had popped into the middle of it, so quickly I hadn't seen any of it before it was all there.

Muffled scratching started again at the big desk, and Gracie's eyes swung without expression from her book to me.

Her fingers began to work at the rolled top of the dingy bag. It opened finally, like a flower, and she tipped it slowly down into the sag of skirt between her legs. There was a small sliding noise.

Her hand put the bag delicately on one knee, and felt into the sagging gingham, and then came very deliberately out into the aisle and toward me.

Mine went as slowly toward it. They met, moistly. And I was left with something that I had expected to wiggle but that instead lay motionless in my folded palm. Of course it wasn't a worm; even Mexicans don't eat worms. I should have known.

It was small and duller than Gracie's, half-clear like the glycerin soap that company had once left in our bathroom, and it was shaped like a tiny cucumber pickle. On one side, that is. On the smooth side were raised letters spelling HEINZ.

I looked at Gracie. She stared at me as if I were a stranger and put a little pickle into her mouth. I did the same with mine.

First it tasted like sweat and dirt, the way my hands tasted before lunch on Saturdays when I'd been playing all morning. Then it tasted smooth. That was all. I could feel the letters on it and the cucumber lumps.

Now was the time to pop it out. I began to move my mouth around. But Gracie was frowning at me. She meant, Wait. I could see that she was sucking on hers. Oh, yes. That was to get the lumps off, so it would slide more easily. I sucked hard, until my cheeks went in between my teeth and my tongue got prickles on it.

The green cucumber was growing smaller, turning into a slick worm. I looked expectantly at Gracie. She sucked once or twice more, and then her mouth began that queer process of shriveling into a purple knot.

Mine felt less round somehow. I wished that I could see it. When I went home I'd practice in the bathroom mirror.

The purple knot began to tremble. Out shot the little worm. In it went, then out, then in again, without a sound.

Gracie looked impassively at me, waiting for my turn.

I sucked once more, nervously. My mouth felt loose and soft, not at all efficient. Gracie frowned slightly. Her worm made a flashing appearance. Now she looked impatient.

The room was silent as a cat. I made my mouth tight, felt the green worm slippery behind my lips—and shot it forth. It hit the primer of John B., The Teacher's Pet, three seats away, and then fell to his desk. I saw the wet marks on his book.

A loud slippery laugh, like a worm but not a green one, suddenly shot out of Gracie's mouth, and in the second before I looked at Miss Newby I saw that the sky was graying so that it would surely be cold on Saturday.

II

After the trouble about the worm and getting John B.'s book dirty, Gracie had to move her seat. She was scolded more than I, too, because she was the worst girl in the first grade and probably in the whole school, and I was so nice.

She cared much less than I did about all the talk and had already been sent out of the room for two other offenses.

Now she had a terrible cold. Ever since the day of the worm, rain had fallen and the wind had blown, and now Gracie coughed like an old and rattling steamroller.

She never stayed out of school, as the rest of us did when we had colds or stomachaches. We all rather enjoyed those too-transient ills. The next day other children would ask us what was the matter, and if we'd been really sick, our mothers would write notes to Miss Newby about letting us eat oranges at recess or making us wear sweaters.

But Gracie won even more attention by spending every day of the year at school. Her mother had too many other children around the house as it was, without any ailing ones.

And of course Gracie was never really sick, as far as we knew, not sick enough for bed and a thermometer as we had all been at least one thrilling time. She only had colds.

Once in a while she put her head on her desk, with great daring, and when Miss Newby asked her rather coldly if she felt tired, she would deny it with brave weariness on every curve of her mocking dark face. We felt that she was sophisticated.

And once she had thrown up on the floor. That was exciting but disagreeable. I felt sorry for the janitor.

Now, however, it was only a cold. But I had never heard one like it, nor have I since.

She was small and rather fat, with square shoulders and a round head covered with straight navy-blue hair with pink cloth woven into the braids, but when she coughed I felt as if she had changed into six baying hound dogs and a big brass horn being blown with rain in it, all at once.

There was something of cracking wood, too, like branches being torn away from a tree, or Father breaking sticks over his knee.

And there was something of the booming of high tide in the hollow cliffs near Woods Point in Laguna.

When Gracie coughed, everything in the room stopped. Miss Newby, if she was reading or talking to us, stopped. If we were singing or reciting or spelling in chorus, we stopped. We stopped even when we weren't doing anything.

Sometimes we looked at Gracie, but as we grew more accustomed to it, we looked away. She was not pretty. She struggled terribly. Her dark face turned darker, and her shiny eyes stuck out with the whites turning red with pressure. She shook.

For a week or two Miss Newby felt sorry for her. She was very nice to a girl who gave her so much trouble, a "bad girl." Everybody said so. She patted her on the back and let her go out for a drink. We'd hear Gracie whooping and booming down in the girls' basement, underneath our room. The sound came up hollow and like a threat of something.

Sometimes she would stay down there too long after she had stopped coughing, and Miss Newby would be ready to go for her, but always as she walked toward the door the noise would start again.

Yes, Miss Newby was very patient. But now we could see that the whole business was getting on her nerves. She jumped as if a door had banged when the cough started, and when it lasted too long she frowned—slightly but unmistakably. Finally she told Gracie that she wanted her to do something about it.

Next day Gracie coughed more than ever. Miss Newby began to look wrinkled and gray, like the time her mother died. She asked Gracie to bring some cough drops to school the next day or else to stay home until her cough was better.

But Gracie came, and her cough was like a truckload of empty oil cans on a bumpy road. Miss Newby pressed her hands to her temples. And then she opened her locked drawer and gave Gracie a nickel for some cough drops.

We all watched silently as Gracie clutched the money and walked toward the door. Going out like that in the middle of the morning was unheard of. We were tight with envy and interest.

She reached the door, turned to Miss Newby, coughed once loudly, and disappeared.

When she came back, at least half an hour later—although we all knew that she had only gone half a block from school to the corner store—she had two boxes of black candy, with two bearded men on the cover of each box. It was pretty good candy.

She gave one piece to me and one to Bertha Wolf, the girl who had fits, and ate the rest. But her cough grew worse.

About half a week later Miss Newby, gray as mold, gave her another nickel. Gracie winked slightly at me as she coughed her way out the door. This time there was only one box, but the candy was better, with a taste of mentholatum.

A week later Gracie was bowed over her desk, her face dark brown and swelling, her fists clenched.

Miss Newby walked to her. I wondered what kind of cough drops Bertha and I would eat at recess. But Miss Newby led her from the room. In a minute we heard a yell from the basement.

Gracie told us at recess that Miss Newby had painted her throat with iodine, but it had taken three teachers to hold her. And true, when she spat, it was a little brown. That was iodine, she said.

III

Gracie was a figure of romance.

For one thing, she was so dirty—not with bad dirt but simply with a different dirt from any I was used to. To see her and smell her made me feel ordinary. I felt ashamed of my dull self. She had a warm rich smell, like manure, while I never smelled anything but clean, except maybe on hot Saturdays before my bath.

But too close to Gracie the smell was less agreeable than manure; it was an odor that made me catch my breath. Now I recognize it as digested garlic, but then I just thought it was Gracie. And even that added to her fascination.

And of course she was brown. Everybody else I knew in the first grade, except Lucille and Alice Lunt, was white or pink, and from what Mother had said I knew that even Lucille and Alice would be like me if they didn't drink coffee. That seemed to tint them.

Gracie wasn't coffee-colored, though. She reminded me more of the living-room floor with fresh polish on it.

Then she had navy-blue hair like so many of the Indian Mexicans. That alone made her romantic.

We talked about her sometimes, although many of the girls were almost embarrassed to. Ardine and Eileen, who loved each other and whose fathers were a mayor and a professor, never said anything about Gracie but only about the girls who did talk of her and to her. They looked at me with some condescension but were nice to me because my father was editor of the town paper.

Jacqueline, the banker's daughter, hated me because I had told her I liked Gracie better than I liked her. She would have liked to be my best friend, but Gracie spoiled it. So she hated me and loved Hazel Montague instead.

Another thing about Gracie was that she was hard, not soft and yielding as we all were in varying degrees. In any of the accidents that happened during recess, the falls and bumps and slivers and skinned knees, I never saw Gracie shiver or squeal or turn faint. Only once did she cry, either, and I made her do that.

It is easy to make children cry, even the strong ones, by singing at them one of those diabolical songs that rise and fall on playgrounds, those songs usually two lines long, sung on two or three notes over and over.

Gracie Meller's name was too fortunate to let pass. Often the song about it would start, in recess or at noon, for no reason except that the children wanted to hop up and down in rhythm, their lungs open. It would grow softly, venomously, like fire in an old house, until the whole playground rocked:

> *Gra-cie Mel-ler*
> *Had-da fel-ler*
> *Gra-cie Mel-ler*
> *Had-da fel-ler—*

At first Gracie pretended not to hear. Her eyes grew watchful and her back straighter, but she seemed to hear nothing.

If it kept up, and it usually did, she ran to the squeakiest swing and pumped high into the air, her skirts flying shockingly above her round, half-naked buttocks.

Sometimes that worked. Gracie was the best girl in school for pumping up, and we watched her always with the horrified feeling that one day she would swing clear over the bar, like a circus performer. But more often the dreadful song rose with her into the air and into her ears with the rushing wind. And she would let the swing die down, her face set.

Still she never cried, as any of us would have done, until the day I made up the variation on our song.

Everybody knew that Mexicans liked red and yellow together, a color combination that froze us with exaggerated disgust. We had a song for it:

Red-and yel-ler
Kiss-your fel-ler—

So, I concluded logically, people who kissed their fellows, a process that was mysteriously vulgar to all of us, must thus be Mexicans.

And one day, when all the girls I knew were singing gently and insidiously in a nasty circle around Gracie, I whispered to Ardine and Eileen,

Red-and yel-ler
Gra-cie Mel-ler
Kissed-her fel-ler
Red-and yel-ler
Gra-cie Mel-ler—

The little girls squealed with joy, and up rose my song like a pagan hymn, over and over.

Finally, Gracie's face, like stone usually, began to pucker and move. Her shiny eyes dropped. I felt terribly uncomfortable and wondered desperately if I was going to begin to cry in front of the other girls. But Gracie did instead.

She broke roughly through the circle of swaying, delighted children and ran toward the girls' basement. I could hear her sobbing angrily, with hard noises.

The girls stopped singing, and Jacqueline muttered something about a crybaby, and then they wandered away. They had already forgotten that I was the poet of the most delightful song of the week, of the year even, but I was miserable for a long time.

Another of the many reasons for Gracie's romance was her mother. Sometimes we would whisper together, four or five of us, about her. Gracie's mother was hard to see. Often we walked past the shack that held so many people (we knew Gracie had at least a dozen brothers and sisters), but we never saw her.

I would tell the little girls about the one time I had walked home with Gracie, and her mother had come to the window.

She was a woman black as a Negro and wide as five white women. Jacqueline, who hated me, asked if she was as wide as my mother, always having babies, too, and the girls gasped. I decided I hated Jacqueline too much to speak to her and went on talking. She was embarrassed.

Gracie's mother had worn her hair, which was black with blue places in it, in a braid, and the braid was in a flat knot on top of her head. The knot was as big as a pie.

Her ears hung down to her shoulders with gold in them, so Gracie must be rich. And her eyes were like Gracie's but no bigger than a parrot's.

She hadn't said a word, just leaned there in the window and looked at me. Gracie had run into the shack without telling me good-bye, either, and I had gone home full of regrets and wonderings about other families.

I did not yet see how any of them could be different from my own and still be called a family. It was hard to realize that my friends all had families when I knew that mine was the only one. There was something imitated about their families—like the paper tulips stuck row after row on the glass of the first-grade windows. I felt irritated at them all, and jealous.

It was some comfort, though, that none of them had a little fat sister named Anne. Gracie, of course, had several fatter ones, but they were less like sisters than round puppies, barking and nipping and rolling in the pressed-down dirt in front of their shack. They urinated against the side of the house like dogs, too.

And their noses ran. Gracie's did even more than theirs. I

thought perhaps it was because she was older—something to do with Mexicans.

The other girls at school had handkerchiefs, which they used with delicacy, like Ardine and Eileen, or with ostentation, like the slightly coarser Hazel Montague. But Gracie sniffed—occasionally.

She never combed her hair, the girls said, shaking their sleek bobbed heads. But I defended her. Every Friday, I reminded them, she came with new braids or at least with water plastering down the front of her cap of thick blue-blackness. Of course it got rather fuzzy in back, where she slept, but Japanese ladies did that, too.

The girls were silent with respect. I had told them a lie about Mother's having lived in Japan for countless years, so I was a recognized authority on things oriental.

But Gracie's hands! Ardine shuddered, and she and Eileen looked proudly at her long pallid fingers. We all knew that her mother took special care of them because Ardine was going to play the piano.

I liked Gracie's short dirty fingers much better. They had a certain pudgy strength in them, and they reminded me of Anne's —a gentle stillness, like the Kewpies' hands in *Good Housekeeping*.

Suddenly I felt very bored by all those little girls in their clean dresses and went off to look for Gracie. She had never said anything about the song I made up, and I knew that although she would not forget it, she still liked me.

She would be scratching faces on the walls of the girls' basement. Or maybe looking through the wire fence by the boys' drinking fountain. Both things were forbidden, and as I went to join her, I wanted to do them, too, yet I still couldn't help praying that Miss Newby would not see me from her window. I loved Gracie and I loved being a nice girl too.

IV

In the second grade and, as I remember, well into the third, we were swept by waves of being pictures.

Today little girls probably have attacks, singly and in groups, of being Shirley Temple, but when Ardine and Eileen and Jacqueline the banker's daughter and her less genteel shadow Hazel Montague and I were in the throes of such periods, we were all of us drawings by Jessie Wilcox Smith.

By that time we were seven or eight years old and not only able to read but capable of cutting out pictures by ourselves. We made scrapbooks of our heroines, "Galleries of Beauty," in which each picture represented our own selves in one guise or another.

We were those roundheaded children with pointed chins and rabbit eyes, those quaint peasant girls and princesses, those merry blank-faced moppets with unreal accoutrements and prissy rosebud mouths.

Fortunately for us, the magazines were well larded with Miss Smith's works, and at least once a month there was a cover by her, a mistily beautiful cover that told such a simple story that even our budding brains could invent elaborations on it.

If two children, the daughters surely of nobility, stood twined with apple blossoms and each other's arms on the cover of *Good Housekeeping,* they were Ardine and Eileen, no others.

Even Gracie Meller, who usually scorned our pictures as silly (Jacqueline whispered spitefully that it was because Gracie had no magazines anyway), even Gracie would look stonily at the picture and then with recognition at the two dainty smirking little white girls who loved each other.

Then she would laugh her strange jeering laugh and go off alone.

Ardine and Eileen, their faces flushed, looked pityingly after her—poor Gracie was *so* common. Their eyes met, understanding and passion burning gently in them. Each sighed rapturously, recognizing herself in the other's prettiness.

They walked off, an aura of apple blossoms and ancestral gems about them, their soft-colored dresses even more mistily lovely than those on the magazine cover.

Jacqueline and Hazel Montague and I were less easily identifiable; still, we managed to fit ourselves, at least to our own satisfaction, into most of the Smith pictures.

We were chubby peasant children sometimes, and I remember how patiently my mother allowed me to dribble milk all over myself, simply because the Smith peasants on the cover drank theirs from round bowls instead of cups.

Or we were especially misty dream children looking for magic birds. That was more difficult, since it was solely a matter of imagination, with not even the comforting prop of a milk bowl.

My little sister Anne was enviously recognized by my friends as the exact counterpart of all the Smith babies: she was round, charming, obviously childlike.

I was proud to have them envy her, but I was already beginning to know that Anne was far from the simple babe she looked. She was emerging in my mind as rather mysterious. I blandly let my friends use her as Jessie Wilcox Smith's silly infant in their pictures, but to myself I identified her firmly with any or all of Rose O'Neill's more uproarious Kewpies. I knew her better than the other girls did.

It was harder to place people like Emma and Evelyn Wolf. (Bertha, who had fits, was never, of course, depicted in Miss Smith's pretty pictures.) The Wolfs were nice children, so quiet, so clean, so unmistakably damned.

They would do anything we wanted, even Emma, who was in the fourth grade and should have had more dignity. It was always

she, or our classmate Evelyn, who played the starved kitchen slave
or the hungry beggar child or any such picture part that was not
too glamorous.

(In the case of Sarah Crewe or a Little Match Girl, though, I
always had first place. I seemed to have a feeling for starvation, for
pressing my cold nose against the window separating me from the
rich children's Christmas tree, that even a thin, cowed Evelyn Wolf
could never imitate.)

Once both the Wolfs were in the same picture, to our intense
jealousy. There they crouched, as real as life, two little pinched
dreary figures with snow swirling around them. Even their funny
twiglike braids of mousy hair were there.

We covered our envy as best we could: by teasing them. But
it wasn't until Jacqueline started singing,

> *Holes* in your *shoes*
> *Holes* in your *shoes*
> *Holes* in your *shoes*

that they cried.

Soon after that the Wolfs' scrapbook began to be much better
than ours. They had pictures we had only seen in books from the
library, sometimes duplicated even, which we eagerly bargained
for.

The two little girls fairly blossomed in the warmth of our
attention: they looked almost happy. Finally they whispered that
Gracie Meller had given them all the pictures, and please not to
tell.

(Of course someone did, but it was not until three years later,
when we had all left Penn Street School, that the city library found
it was Gracie who had stripped all the Jessie Wilcox Smith illustra-

tions from its books. She was suspended, for that and several other reasons, from the public schools.)

Except for one pang I felt, to think that Gracie would give pictures to the Wolfs when she might have offered them to me, I almost forgot her for a while. My whole life was a series of Smith pictures, and Gracie, so blunt, so—yes, I must agree for once with Ardine and Eileen—so *common,* was hardly a picture person.

Filled as we all were with visions of ourselves as glamorously dark-eyed or fairylike heroines, Gracie's square strong body and her coarse hair were distasteful to us. And her manners went ill with our dreamy floatings about the school yard. She became less real to us than the pictures we lived.

One night, however, I reached the peak of this fatuous existence and have never been able to resume any part of it since (as far as I know).

The last cover of *Good Housekeeping* had shown a lovely Smith child saying her prayers. She knelt, her body dimly outlined under the quaint white nightgown, before an open window. Two little pink feet peeked from the ripples of white, two little hands folded piously, and the lovely misty head, candle lighted, was bent and yet somehow managed to lift two deep blue eyes to the starry blackness of the night.

It was a warm night. I knelt before the open window. My nightie was striped and rather short, but from the street my feet might well be imagined as peeking, pink and tiny, from folds of white.

And of course there was no candlelight behind me. I had arranged the door, though, to let in a glow from the upstairs hall.

I raised my eyes to the dark sky. I had never prayed and certainly never on my knees with my hands clasped, but that night I asked God fervently to send someone along the street, someone who would look up and say to himself, "Oh, how exquisite—a lovely child at prayer, just like the cover of the last *Good House-keeping!*"

Suddenly I leapt up and into bed and far under the covers. I was shaken with horror and embarrassment. What, *what* if Gracie Meller should see me! What would Gracie, so simple, so straight, think of me? My ears rang with her hard laughter.

The next day I tried to give my scrapbook of fair princesses and dreamy peasant children to Anne, and when she wouldn't take it, I threw it away.

V

In the first grade, when we sang "Red and yellow, kiss your fellow," it meant final damnation. The color combination was considered thoroughly bad, and for that reason, perhaps, kissing your fellow was, too. We never thought much about it, one way or the other, although we knew that when we grew up, probably in the third grade, we would have fellows. Maybe we would kiss them, but—sufficient unto the day was the evil thereof.

When Ardine and Eileen and Jacqueline and her toady Hazel Montague and Gracie Meller and I were in the second grade, though, we were rudely thrown into a drama of passion, long before our time. It was because of my little sister Anne.

Anne was in the first grade by then, and that was one of the worst things about the whole exciting business. At Penn Street School nobody *ever* had a fellow before she was in the third grade, and there Anne was, madly in love and hardly out of kindergarten.

When I first heard about it, I was shocked.

> *Anne*'s got a *fel*-low,
> *Anne*'s got a *fel*-low,
> *Anne*'s got a *fel*-low,

Jacqueline sang it gleefully at me, and her friend Hazel giggled rather apprehensively.

"Who? *My* Anne? She—has—*not!*" I was furious, as if someone had made a lewd remark about her, which indeed it almost was, then.

But it was hard to deny the truth in Jacqueline's malicious song much longer. The whole school soon knew about Anne and Thomas.

I never mentioned it to my sister. She suddenly seemed much older than I, and I did not feel hurt or reproachful but only moved, as I do now at the little I can remember of the affair.

The teachers did, too. At first they were amused, and then they were touched and strangely upset, and fortunately the whole thing died before they could feel alarm or irritation.

Anne and Thomas were drawn together like two rare animals or insects who, alone of their kind in a great forest, find each other for love. They looked alike, small fat merry things with dark eyes and fine dark hair. They both had four dimples on the back of each hand.

As soon as recess began, they would meet at the wire fence that separated the boys from the girls and stand close to each other. Sometimes they would kiss, delicately, on cheek or mouth. Usually they embraced by pressing their small dimpled hands palm to palm. They spoke little and looked at each other without smiling.

It was strange and mysterious to see my sister so quiet. I was not surprised, though. I wanted to protect her, not possessively for once, but almost religiously.

Of course, everyone could see her at recess, standing brazenly with Thomas, and sometimes at the beginning of the affair the older girls would draw into a group near them.

Then I would lure my friends away by starting a game of tag

or daring one or another to pump up in the swings. Gracie Meller seemed to know what I was doing, and between us we usually managed to keep a clear space around the lovers.

(It wouldn't have mattered about an audience, probably. I doubt if anything could have shattered their intensity. They were drowned in each other.)

When the girls teased me about Anne, I could only beat them at their own game, because although they didn't have fellows, I knew enough about almost every girl to be able to flick her private scars.

We none of us had felt love yet, and Anne disturbed us. She and her lover soon parted, as easily and unknowingly as they had come together, and she seemed the same as before. The rest of us, though—and probably the teachers, too—were changed.

We could never say "fellow" again with the same fine first-grade scorn. We could never again be quite oblivious to boys; from now on, willy-nilly, we must wonder if every one we met could be our own fellow.

In the third grade we found out. I forget about the other girls —they probably had fellows, too—but I know I fell in love with Red Somerville.

I can't remember much about Red, except that he was tall and rakish, one of the "bad boys" and one I had never noticed in the two years I sat next to him. The beginning and the end are gone from my mind, but I know I really loved him for a time, and he me.

My affair was not as pure as my little sister's, because it was more worldly. I was older, and for a few months Red and I were the darlings of the sophisticated element of Penn Street.

We were more daring on roller skates, we could run faster on our long legs, we could spit drinking water further than any other boy and girl. Separated, we were perhaps a little above average; together we were breathtaking. And I loved my glamorous new life almost as much as I did Red, which was a great deal.

I never touched him. Our whole affair was taciturn, like a modern comedy. Once I kissed my hand to him, behind his back, but only because Jacqueline dared me to in such an insulting way that I had to do it or kill her.

He used to give me presents, though.

He started with the gold stars from his spelling and arithmetic papers (he was a good student and earned lots of them).

Then, as he grew to know my tastes better, he managed somehow to buy me things that were forbidden at home: jawbreakers, licorice whips, ghastly little marshmallow bananas that I was sure must be delicious because Mother had told me they were made of unmentionable stuff.

Red and I reached one of our highest moments as Penn Street's most popular couple when he gave me, in public this time instead of nonchalantly leaving it on my desk as he usually did, the first five-cent candy bar that any of us had ever seen.

It was called a Cherry Flip, I think, and was a large lump of pink cream around a red cherry, with thick knobbed chocolate on the outside.

The thought that Red had spent a whole nickel on me was almost more than I could stand. I insisted that he take half of the candy, but even then I felt rather awed. I knew he loved me, perhaps more than I did him.

I gave a decent-sized bite of the Cherry Flip to Gracie. She had always been generous with me, the few times she had cough drops or a stick of gum or some fruit. I felt sorry for her. There we all were, lapped in love, and Gracie was out of it because she was a Mexican. If there had been any dark-skinned boys at Penn, she would probably have had a flirtation; even sturdy Gracie could not have withstood the lovesickness that hit us in the third grade. But as it was, she walked alone.

After the Christmas holidays, there must have been some cooling in my feelings for Red, because when a new boy came to school I was very conscious of him.

His name was Luke Bartholomew. It was such a beautiful name that I felt sure he would fall in love with me. (Now I can't follow that reasoning, but then it seemed obvious.)

Luke, though, fell in love with nobody. He may have loved God or Jesus—he had a faraway look always, as if he were listening to a voiceless song, and he often smiled at friends who were invisible.

He had few visible ones, certainly. He was too far away from us. On the playground there was always a space around him. He was taller than most of the boys, and when he walked to the school door or the toilets, he seemed to glide a little above the ground.

He had large eyes with rings under them, a dead white skin, and cinnamon-colored hair, which he wore longer than the other boys', in soft curls all over his head.

We were much interested in him, and I at least would have renounced all my exciting races and my Cherry Flips for his attentions.

It was a long time before I realized that Gracie Meller felt that way, too. She said nothing, of course, and probably it never occurred to any of the others. To them, Gracie was Mexican; that automatically canceled any normal "white" reactions to Luke's strange beauty.

I noticed that Gracie had stopped playing with us. She often played alone anyway, because Ardine and Eileen and some of the others were nice to her only when they felt like it. Now none of them missed her.

But it seemed queer to me that she always did the same thing, instead of pumping up one recess and hurling herself around the Giant Stride another as she used to. Now she went straight to the camphor tree by the fence and climbed it quickly to the most hidden branch, because we were forbidden to go into the trees. From there she watched Luke Bartholomew, standing alone on the boys' side. That was all. She did it every recess from New Year's, when he drifted into our school, until he drifted away from us again.

That was on Valentine's Day. I remember because we always had a box, gaudy with red hearts and ruffles of crepe paper, into which we put valentines for friends and which we opened on the afternoon of February 14.

The teacher usually gave us each a little sugar heart, and the day was quite gay in spite of the sadness of children who got only one valentine and the mock surprise of favorites who got piles of them.

"It is too bad," the third-grade teacher said, "that Luke Bartholomew could not be here one more day for our party. He has gone away."

I looked quickly at Gracie, but she was imperturbable. Perhaps I had imagined that she loved him?

That afternoon the valentines were distributed, we thanked our teacher for her candies, and then we counted what we had been given.

As always, the children who were socially and physically strong got most of the cards, and little forlorn girls like Evelyn Wolf were grateful for one or two of the cheapest ones.

Any discomfort I felt at their pitiable gratitude was almost wiped out, that year, by my getting more than anybody else, even Jacqueline. I think now that Red Somerville saw to that, disguising his handwriting several times on the envelopes.

The only one he admitted putting into the box for me, though, was the first and last one I ever got that had several layers. Each layer was on paper springs, so that when I unbent them a little, the whole beautiful lacy thing was inches deep.

It was a ten-minute marvel. Everybody gathered around my desk, where it lay, and I glowed with gratitude to Red for it and for my popularity.

Even at that age, though, I knew I should at least pretend to be interested in other people. Before the wonder of Red's valentine had waned, I went to look at the other girls' displays, especially generous with my admiration since I had received more than any of them.

I looked at Gracie's last. Most of my friends were tired by then, and only Jacqueline and I were at her desk.

She showed us her sparse collection, and we guessed who each one was from.

"Who sent that one?" Jacqueline asked scornfully of the last card. It was unusually flimsy, with writing on the back.

When Gracie didn't answer, Jacqueline picked it up and then exclaimed, "Luke Bartholomew! Why, he didn't send any to the rest of us!"

Gracie laughed jeeringly and said, "Oh, he's crazy!"

As soon as we went away, I saw her put her head down on the desk, and I knew that the way she loved Luke Bartholomew was much different from Red Somerville and me, or even Thomas and my little sister Anne.

VI

It seems strange to me that anyone as important as Gracie could be lost so soon from my life. I never saw her again after I was maybe fourteen, and only twice more after I was nine.

I remember once she came to the house when I was nine or ten, and my mother did not like her. She was probably a little jealous of her because I had once asked her why I could not have beautiful brown skin like Gracie, and she had replied crossly that nobody nice had brown skin. And she had held me close to her, and I could feel her heart beating through her great white breasts, and she had said sadly to me that I would always be pink and white and that I should thank God for it. I didn't ask her why, but I felt very protective of her for the first time in my life, and I felt sorry for her, too.

Soon after that Gracie came to our house, along with Ardine and Eileen and two other nice white girls, and we ate bowlsful of cornflakes and milk and sugar, kneeling on the floor around the piano bench. Gracie was very messy, and I could tell that Mother was cross with all of us but especially Gracie, and we never did it again.

Then once about a year later, the first of two embarrassing moments happened when I found myself standing in front of our house on North Painter Avenue with Gracie and four or five friends. We all boasted that we had fathers who made more money than Gracie's father. Gracie became very ashamed and did not deny it, and we were laughing at her and I began to feel bad. Then Gracie said that she had no father, and all the other girls laughed at her. I laughed, too, and said that my father made more money than any of them. Jacqueline, the banker's daughter, argued with me a little, and my voice got very loud and I said that my father earned at least fifteen dollars a day, and we all broke up and Gracie went away without saying another word.

I felt ashamed about this, and as far as I know we never mentioned money again.

We soon moved to the country, and my years were very happy there. But when I was fourteen, I went to school in Whittier again, because I was the editor's daughter and I had to try anything new, which in this case was the intermediate school between grammar and high school called John Muir. It was for the seventh and eighth grades. I was in the eighth grade and suddenly I was supposed to be grown-up.

The first day I went to school it had been going on for about six weeks, and I felt out of place and shy. I had a grown-up dress on, made of a nubby ratiné cloth that was stylish then. It was a hand-me-down from a rich cousin in Pittsburgh, and I had looked forward to wearing it. It was bright orange with black binding around the neck and sleeves, and it had a wide black belt of silk down around my hips. I was a tall skinny girl, slab-sided and shapeless, and when I put the dress on, I knew at once it was unbecoming.

I hated everything about having to go to school in town again, and I went alone to the playground for recess. There, suddenly, was Gracie. We greeted each other like old friends, and we went together to a far corner and started talking almost hungrily. She told me of her two older brothers who were in the pen together at San Quentin and that she was leaving that night forever, to live near them. It all sounded very exciting to me, and I longed to go with her. Instead, I said that I might go to South America with my uncle, or I might go back to Ann Arbor, Michigan, to live with my aunt. I added that my mother did not approve of my aunt because she thought that I might turn into a social butterfly.

"What is a social butterfly?" Gracie asked rudely, and she glared at me and then laughed harshly and walked away.

I watched her straight blue-black hair hanging down, and I knew that I would never see her again. I knew that I was damned forever to be pink and white, as my mother had told me several years before, and I felt like crying. I still do now and then when I think of Gracie, and I wish that I had never told her that my father made more money then her father ever could, and that we lived in a bigger house, and all that nonsense about social butterflies. And I wonder what ever happened to her. I hope that if she is alive she does not remember me.

—1957, 1991

13
My Family's Escape Hatch:
A Reminiscence
(1915–1926)

San Francisco has been my family's escape hatch for at least sixty-five years, our favorite prescription for everything from blues to blahs to plain animal bliss, and in spite of some current suspicions that the city may be trying to imitate the overcrowded evil confusion of many other great spiritual watering holes, it continues to be our help in times of uneasiness.

I first learned of San Francisco's magic in 1915 when I was going on six and my father and mother went on a wild spree northward from Whittier, California, to visit the Panama Pacific Exposition. They arranged to meet their favorite friend there, Mother's brother Evans, a young law professor fairly fresh out of Stanford. He had been sent there to get him as far as possible from the East Coast and the Midwest, where he had been firmly expelled from three universities for merrymaking.

The three of them had what was called, in our family lingo, "a fine old time," which means that they felt completely carefree and rather silly and slightly tipsy for at least the week they were there. Plainly, they forgot small children and duties and classes and getting the *Whittier News* out on time, and frolicked giddily from one beautiful thing to another in what many people have said was one of the most enchanting fairs seen by man.

When Mother and Father came home, they brought my younger sister Anne and me two little cardboard suitcases covered —as was then the fashion—with imitation hotel stickers from all over the world.

They were easy to open, just like what were called satchels or "grips" in those days. And they were filled to their tops with souvenirs, always one for each of us, from almost every display in the great fair. There were swizzle sticks and matchboxes, tiny Japanese fans and theater programs. There were even two sugar cubes from the Garden Court of the Palace Hotel, hand-wrapped in thin Chinese paper, and cable-car passes and postcards.

After Anne and I had laid out every exotic mystery and been told its what and why, we packed them away again neatly and set out to show all the neighbors on our side of the block on North Painter where our parents had been. I don't know if Mother telephoned ahead, but everyone seemed delighted to see us and invited us in to show them the contents of our little satchels. And nobody asked us for even a wee bar of Ghirardelli chocolate.

Mr. Fay, five houses up, pretended that we were selling something. He almost closed the door on us, very grumpily, until he seemed to recognize us. This was somewhat unsettling, but we pulled ourselves together and let him choose a postcard of an open taxicab rolling decorously through Golden Gate Park between banks of bright pink flowers, with two ladies carrying open parasols to match. Mr. Fay said that all women in San Francisco were equally beautiful and stylish. We were sure he was right, because he was from Boston.

By the time Anne and I, in a week or so, had nibbled our way through everything in our treasure bags, we knew a surprising lot about the wondrous city, filled with palaces and opium dens and lying like a seductive arm along the edge of the world, with the wild Pacific on one side and the wide quiet bay on the other. We even knew what opium was. We learned about rex sole—obviously named, in some way, for our father, Rex Kennedy—and about sand dabs. Father said the latter were the most delicate fish in the world, especially as served at Sam's, but Mother stood up for rex sole meunière, because of her husband's name and because Uncle Evans had found it at Jack's to be even better than the pompano at Antoine's in New Orleans, wherever that was.

When we were not much older, we learned to look for the big billboard of an enormous bright parrot with a moving head, just before the red Pacific Electric cars brought us into downtown Los Angeles on our occasional shopping sprees for things still unknown in Whittier. The bird was telling us, "Say Gear-ar-dell-y," but we would feel very sophisticated because we already knew that from our tiny samples. (We also knew how to pronounce Dröste, from another delicious little sample our thoughtful parents had gathered for us, but we were too courteous or naive to say, then anyway, which we preferred.)

A few years later we went for a birthday or some other family fiesta to the Victor Hugo in Los Angeles, and Father found sand dabs on the menu. After learning that they had come down that morning on the Lark from San Francisco, he ordered them for all of us. Mother found them delicious, but not as good as the rex sole at Jack's, and it was several more years before Anne and I could judge them for ourselves.

In 1924 we were sent up to Palo Alto to boarding school, and when I was a senior my sister and I were allowed to go several times to the city without a chaperon. We felt like gypsy queens. The first thing we always did was to stop at the flower stand just off Geary by Union Square for blossoms for our left shoulders. The old man pretended to know us and had a magical trick of folding out the petals of a fresh tulip to make it seem as big as a butter plate. We felt infinitely stylish and carefree and silly and even tipsy. Although we did not yet know fully what that meant, we knew exactly where we were, because we had been there before —through those little satchels of souvenirs of the exposition, almost our whole lives before.

Of course, Anne and I never went to restaurants on our wicked little Saturdays; we preferred the Golden Pheasant or some long-forgotten tearoom. The theaters, though, seemed familiar to us when, with a chosen few other students (thoroughly chaperoned, of course), we saw people like John Drew and Jane Cowl and Pavlova at the Geary and the Curran and the even dustier old place on Powell. We'd really been there before, with Father and Mother and Uncle Evans; now we always saved our own theater programs to give to our own still-undreamed-of children.

When either of our parents came up from Whittier to see us for a weekend, which they found a surprising number of excuses to do, we stayed at one of the small hotels where Rex as an editor had a due bill, but we knew exactly what the elegant Palace Hotel would look like, from our old postcards, and felt immediately at home in its airy grandeur. And when Mother escaped from southern California now and then, with her two poor homesick starving daughters as a fairly feeble excuse, we always lunched at least once in the Garden Court. We knew its vast atrium by heart, from the first days when fine carriages pranced into it until that very noon. There were no more hand-wrapped sugar cubes, but we always ate a legendary salad whose name I forget (*not* a Green Goddess, although that was good, too); it was a kind of pyramid of tiny crisp shrimps and finely cut pale tender lettuce, set on a monumental artichoke heart as wide as a baseball.

Mother said that the melba toast there was the best she had ever eaten, the thinnest and most intelligent—which from her was a rare accolade. Once we were taken down into the kitchens to smile and bow at an ancient Chinese who sat at a special little table cutting long loaves of bread by hand for the toast. He was very small and did not smile or miss a stroke of his long knife. Some twenty years later, when I was in San Francisco alone, writing about all the young soldiers heading from there to the South Pacific, I went down again to the cellars. The white-tiled walls remained, but the cooks stood on raised wooden gratings to avoid the kind of mess of spillings we had tried to ignore the first time. The ancient man still sat there slicing bread. He looked even smaller and did not smile, but his knife went up and down in the same careful rhythm.

In the twenties, Prohibition was firmly in sway around Los Angeles, but in San Francisco there always seemed to be whatever one wanted to drink, and my parents obviously did not suffer when they both came up to share the escape hatch with us. When Mother came alone, of course she would not dream of drinking either privately or in public with two young ladies, but with her husband alongside we drank wines in good restaurants. They were often served from tall, dark green soda-water bottles and poured into dark glasses. Anne and I were not interested, past the first polite sip. A few times the older people sat after a long lunch over liqueurs brought to the table in demitasse cups, and my sister and I were excused and went off to prowl, innocent and unbothered, around Union Square's side streets.

In my senior year, Uncle Evans spent his sabbatical from the University of Michigan at Stanford, and he had once introduced us to old Mr. Gump, so we felt all right about snooping from top to bottom of his store, of course with permission. Mother knew a few shops in Chinatown where we could pass easily from the front to the secret back and look with awe at the beautiful things behind all the shoddy junk put out for tourists. And Union Square itself was a place of bright windy spaces and ever-changing miracles of flowers and trees, with fine sweeps of lawn and sedate old men sitting on benches. I don't remember any signs saying "KEEP OFF," but nobody ever lay down on the green grass or threw litter there or fell down and threw up. It, too, was innocent, like us.

Marriages and divorces and deaths and births happened in our family, of course, but San Francisco stayed firmly in our credo as the cure, the salve and balm, the escape hatch. We fled there singly, or in twos and threes when sadness or ennui threatened us. Now and then we even lived there, but every minute seemed always a kind of *event*—to breathe deeply of the clean cool air, to look at a long perspective up to a known hill, to feel the four o'clock fog sweep eastward from beyond the Cliff House.

And when I lived about two hours northward with my young girls and had to go down often with them for long painful sessions with their orthodontist, it was still an adventure. It still made us feel carefree and silly and slightly tipsy, just as our parents and Uncle Evans had felt in 1915 when they brought back to us two little mysterious magic kits, all printed over with hotel stickers from Florence and Paris and London and Heidelberg and a dozen other far fair cities we would seek out later for ourselves. But first, and I honestly think, forever, the little satchels brought us San Francisco, the fairest and most magical of them all—and the most healing.

—1983

14
The Broken Chain
(1920)

There has been more talk than usual lately about the abuse and angry beating of helpless people, mostly children and many women. I think about it. I have never been beaten, so empathy is my only weapon against the ugliness I know vicariously. On the radio someone talks about a chain of violence. When is it broken? he asks. How?

When I was growing up, I was occasionally spanked and always by my father. I often had to go upstairs with him when he came home from the *News* for lunch, and pull down my panties and lay myself obediently across his long bony knees, and then steel my emotions against the ritualistic whack of five or eight or even ten sharp taps from a wooden hairbrush. They were counted by my age, and by nine or ten he began to use his hand, in an expert upward slap that stung more than the hairbrush. I often cried a little, to prove that I had learned my lesson.

I knew that Rex disliked this duty very much, but that it was part of being Father. Mother could not or would not punish us. Instead, she always said, by agreement with him and only when she felt that things were serious enough to drag him into it, that she would have to speak with him about the ugly matter when he came home at noon.

This always left me a cooling-off period of thought and regret and conditioned dread, even though I knew that I had been the cause, through my own stupidity, of involving both my parents in the plot.

Maybe it was a good idea. I always felt terrible that it was dragged out. I wished that Mother would whack me or something and get it over with. And as I grew older I resented having to take several undeserved blows because I was the older child and was solemnly expected to be a model to my younger sister, Anne. She was a comparatively sickly child, and spoiled and much cleverer than I, and often made it bitterly clear to me that I was an utter fool to take punishment for her own small jaunty misdoings. I continued to do this, far past the fatherly spankings and other parental punishments, because I loved her and agreed that I was not as clever as she.

Once Rex hit me. I deserved it, because I had vented stupid petulance on my helpless little brother David. He was perhaps a year old, and I was twelve. We'd all left the lunch table for the living room and had left him sitting alone in his high chair, and Father spotted him through the big doors and asked me to get him down. I felt sulky about something, and angered, and I stamped back to the table and pulled up the wooden tray that held the baby in his chair, and dumped him out insolently on the floor. David did not even cry out, but Rex saw it and in a flash leapt across the living room toward the dining table and the empty high chair and gave me a slap across the side of my head that sent me halfway across the room against the big old sideboard. He picked up David and stood staring at me. Mother ran in. A couple of cousins came, looking flustered and embarrassed at the sudden ugliness.

I picked myself up from the floor by the sideboard, really raging with insulted anger, and looked disdainfully around me and then went silently up the stairs that rose from the dining room to all our sleeping quarters. Behind me I could hear Mother crying, and then a lot of talk.

I sat waiting for my father to come up to the bedroom that Anne and I always shared, from her birth until I was twenty, in our two family homes in Whittier, and in Laguna in the summers, and then when we went away to three different schools. I knew I was going to be punished.

Finally Father came upstairs, looking very tired. "Daughter," he said, "your mother wants you to be spanked. You have been bad. Pull down your panties and lie across my knees."

I was growing very fast and was almost as tall as I am now, with small growing breasts. I looked straight at him, not crying, and got into the old position, all long skinny arms and legs, with my bottom bared to him. I felt insulted and full of fury. He gave me twelve expert upward stinging whacks. I did not even breathe fast, on purpose. Then I stood up insolently, pulled up my sensible Munsingwear panties, and stared down at him as he sat on the edge of my bed.

"That's the last time," he said.

"Yes," I said. "And you hit me."

"I apologize for that," he said, and stood up slowly, so that once again I had to look up into his face as I had always done. He went out of the room and downstairs, and I stayed alone in the little room under the eaves of the Ranch house, feeling my insult and anger drain slowly out and away forever. I knew that a great deal had happened, and I felt ashamed of behaving so carelessly toward my helpless little brother and amazed at the way I had simply blown across the room and into the sideboard under my own father's wild stinging blow across my cheek. I wished that I would be maimed, so that he would feel shame every time he looked at my poor face. I tried to forget how silly I'd felt, baring my pubescent bottom to his heavy dutiful slaps across it. I was full of scowling puzzlements.

My mother came into the room, perhaps half an hour later, and wrapped her arms around me with a tenderness I had never felt from her before, although she had always been quietly free with her love and her embraces. She had been crying but was very calm with me, as she told me that Father had gone back to the *News* and that the cousins were playing with the younger children. I wanted to stay haughty and abused with her, but sat there on the bed quietly, while she told me about Father.

She said that he had been beaten when he was a child and then as a growing boy, my age, younger, older. His father beat him, almost every Saturday, with a long leather belt. He beat all four of his boys until they were big enough to tell him that it was the last time. They were all of them tall strong people, and Mother said without any quivering in her voice that they were all about sixteen before they could make it clear that if it ever happened again, they would beat their father worse than he had ever done it to them.

He did it, she said, because he believed that he was ridding them of the devil, of sin. Grandfather, she said quietly, was not a brute or a beast, not sinful, not a devil. But he lived in the wild prairies and raised strong sons to survive, as he had, the untold dangers of frontier life. When he was starting his family, as a wandering newspaperman and printer of political broadsides, he got religion. He was born again. He repented of all his early wildness and tried to keep his four sons from "sinning," as he came to call what he had done before he accepted God as his master.

I sat close to Mother as she explained to me how horrible it had been only a few minutes or hours before in my own short life, when Rex had broken a long vow and struck his own child in unthinking anger. She told me that before they married, he had told her that he had vowed when he was sixteen to break the chain of violence and that never would he strike anyone in anger. She must help him. They promised each other that they would break the chain. And then today he had, for the first time in his whole life, struck out, and he had struck his oldest child.

I could feel my mother trembling. I was almost overwhelmed by pity for the two people whom I had betrayed into this by my stupidity. "Then why did he hit me?" I almost yelled suddenly. She said that he hardly remembered doing it, because he was so shocked by my dumping the helpless baby out onto the floor. "Your father does not remember," she repeated. "He simply had to stop you, stop the unthinking way you acted toward a helpless baby. He was . . . He suddenly acted violently. And it is dreadful for him now to see that, after so long, he can be a raging animal. He thought it would never happen. That is why he has never struck any living thing in anger. Until today."

We talked for a long time. It was a day of spiritual purging, obviously. I have never been the same—still stupid but never unthinking, because of the invisible chains that can be forged in all of us, without our knowing it. Rex knew of the chain of violence that was forged in him by his father's whippings, brutal no matter how mistakenly committed in the name of God. I learned of what violence could mean as I sat beside my mother, that day when I was twelve, and felt her tremble as she put her arm over my skinny shoulders and pulled me toward her in an embrace that she was actually giving to her husband.

It is almost certain that I stayed aloof and surly, often, in the next years with my parents. But I was never spanked again. And I know as surely as I do my given name that Rex no longer feared the chain of violence that had bound him when he was a boy. Perhaps it is as well that he hit me, the one time he found that it had not been broken for him.

—1983

15
Consider the End
(1920)

In Scotland once, mid snow and ice,
A youth did bear this strong device:
Avise la fin!

It was a clan call, albeit in Norman French, and the youth was one of my father's ancestors, and the device said with blunt Scotch economy, Consider the end!

That is what my father did, gastronomically as well as in several other ways, for his offspring. He wanted us to taste life in the round, with all of our senses as well as our wits to work for us. He considered the art of eating a basic part of the plan. He was ably abetted by my mother, a voluptuous woman who had a fine teaching hand with pastry and custards when she cared to and who managed to be assisted, for all I know of her life, by a series of devoted sluggards who may have forgotten to dust beneath the beds but who could produce a dramatic cheese puff for Saturday lunch or a prune tart worthy of any bishop, with children helping and learning under their feet. My father sat back, well nourished and watching, and his clan had little idea that he was considering at least one more end of human fulfillment.

It was sometimes hard, however, to consider the end of our purely gastronomic development when I was little, because of Grandmother's dietetic and emotional strictures, but soon after she died, Father hired a spare little virago he called Anita-Patita. The chef of King Alfonso of Spain had taught her a great deal, she told us, simpering. She spent five days at a time making one meal of enchiladas. She spent three days making a flan, a kind of caramel custard. This casual dismissal of clock and calendar fascinated us children. Nothing must interrupt Anita-Patita's creative concentration. Mother could sit tapping her foot for a few dry diapers for the last batch of babies or waiting to hear the piano under our heavy hands; Father could stop everything but the presses of his newspaper to dash over to North Spring Street in Los Angeles for some correct tortillas and an ounce of the right chili powder: Anita-Patita would move like an imperturbable cricket about the kitchen, reliving other giddier days, no doubt, while my sister and I watched, listened, sliced a tomato or beat an egg, and measured one trembly tablespoon of this or that.

Anita-Patita served her enchiladas with inestimable flourish and pride. She usually neglected to prepare anything else, in her creative flush, but all of us—even Mother, who was suspicious of all exotic flavors as well as domestic melodrama—ate them with both relish and respect. We were indulging in a kind of rebellion from Grandmother's digestive Puritanism, and we permitted ourselves indecorous enthusiasm, at least enough to send the little lonesome scornful Spanish woman back to the kitchen, cackling happily.

There was nothing on the table, besides what plates and silver my sister and I had hastily laid there, but the great steaming platter of delicately rolled tortillas (*we* had helped roll them), with fine chicken in them (which *we* had helped boil and slice), and the big bowl of salsa (our *own* salsa). Father, the boy from Iowa whose ancestors had once cried savagely in the Scotch crags, "Consider the end!," picked up with unexpected skill the fist rolled pancake of fine cornmeal and showed us how to be deft about the dipping and biting and so on. He was preparing us.

Mother forgot that for many hours the usual duties had been ignored and that the table did not look as "set" as she had been trained to see it and that there seemed to be not even a salad. She forgot to tell us to sit up and keep our elbows down.

And then Anita-Patita glided into the room with clean plates and a beautiful flan, so bland and perfect after the hot salsa, and a pot of coffee "black as hell, hot as love, strong as death." And we brought down one of the babies who was chirping, and my sister steeled herself to sing a song about "I saw a little dewdrop," and everything was really fine.

The Spaniard went on her way, as good cooks mostly do. But Father had broken at least a part of the web of cautiousness that Grandmother had spun with her gastronomic asceticism, and from then on we had a series of cooks who did everything from receiving an excessive number of male callers to relieving us of the family silver for worthy causes but who managed, drunk or sober, to tolerate the watching children in the kitchen and to slap amazing victuals on the table whenever the occasion arose, once or twice daily.

All the time my father observed our epicurean education. Consider the end, his face and shoulders said. Dozens of young ones in addition to his own ate their way past him, the big man always at "his" end of the table, always The Carver, always savoring and listening. He shaped us—and, through us, our own children—into a pattern of deliberate and discerning enjoyment.

I know that I still put tortillas over a hot grill or griddle the way I watched Anita-Patita do so long ago. And I know that I would never use cheap oil for the beginnings of a salsa like hers, or an elaborate French sauce, or even for a plain old sauce like Aunt Emma's "receipt" for giblet gravy. And I know, by now, that my own children will never accept haste or suspicion or adulteration in their own ways of sustaining the breath within them. This is because they have seen how not to. They have eaten, as well as cooked, with intelligence since they could hold a spoon, and they have absorbed much more than food over a bowl of good soup.

It is very hard, for more of us than seems possible, to keep some sort of steady serenity in our present noisy mechanized way of life. But I know what strengths I have drawn on, from things like my parents' acceptance of Anita-Patita's slaphappy creations, and I have tried to pass some of it along.

—1958

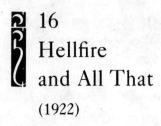

16
Hellfire
and All That
(1922)

It is not clear that I really saw Billy Sunday, the evangelist, standing up in the bandstand in Bailey Street Park and shouting insults for all of us against the God-defying Huns. That would have been in about 1918. Perhaps it was one of his many mimics, who toured the far hinterlands of America in his wake, copying his forceful noisy style. I seem to remember the real "him" though: a strong, wide man, with fists like hams that clenched in the air and trembled with wrath or pounded the Bible as he roared jointly about hellfire and brimstone, and Liberty bonds.

It is strange that my dignified grandmother listened to such crass ranting, but she felt it was "in a good cause," no doubt, and it got me out from underfoot at home to go with her into the green shade of the park and listen, sitting beside her on a bench, while the Billy Sunday brother gave us a good free Christian show.

That was in Whittier, California, when we lived on Painter

Avenue. Life was exciting and rich for me then. Everybody I knew seemed to love me, and that was all I needed. Things were even more interesting after we moved down to the Ranch, out on what was called Painter Extension because it was in the country and not the town. It was like living in Whittier, but across all moats, over all bridges, so that we knew about the town but were no longer of it. We were out of bounds. It made everything more intense. And it was there that I became aware that people love other people, not only as parents and children, but otherwise as well.

Then Grandmother died. I was sorry when one day I found my mother weeping on the living-room couch while the old woman lay in her bedroom with a nurse beside her, softly breathing off and away. But I was puzzled, too. Why weep? I had the detached lack of curiosity of any normal young animal about tears and departures, and it was fine not to have the old lady anymore at the dining-room table.

Grandmother would never have tolerated Rose as our maid-of-all-work, so it was well that she died when she did, a few months before Rose came. Rose stayed at the Ranch for several years, partly because she liked Mother but mostly because her friend Billy could come to the Ranch on Sundays and not be alone in Los Angeles.

Rose was a very tough person, one of the toughest I have ever known, and the first. She had been a hardworking hustler since she was sold to a lumber camp as kitchen help when she was thirteen. Her language was simple and foul. She was complex and ferociously clean. She worked like a horse, keeping us well fed and the shabby old Ranch house sparkling. She was close-mouthed about her past life, but once, when Mother told her she was sorry to add to Rose's chores by inviting two cousins to stay with us for a few weeks, Rose said firmly, "Listen, Miz Kennedy! Get this straight! Bein' here with you and the Mister and your goddamn kids is the best life I ever had. How'd *you* like to work thirty tricks a night and then clean toilets all day! How'd *you*—"

"Yes, Rose. Yes . . ."

The two women got along well. They both had dark eyes and hair. Mother was tall and had once been willowy, a perfect Gibson girl, although by the time I first really looked at her she was hung with an indolent heaviness. Rose was short and square, built close to the ground, as tight as a saddle that is broadening with wear. They respected each other. Once when Anne and I told Mother that Rose had been cross with us in the kitchen, she said that we must always be nice to our cook because she had never been happy. And another time, Rose added a line that still lives in our family collection of favorite quotations, when Mother told her that next week she would have to take down all the curtains and wash them. Rose stood like stone for a minute, her eyes snapping. Then she said flatly, "Now get this, Miz Kennedy, and get it straight. There is only one goddamn thing in this world that Rose *has* to do, and that's die." She stamped out of the room: nothing was ever said about her dictum, and from then on my mother minded her tongue.

She did tell Rose, early on, not to use a few of her saltier words in front of Anne and me, and I am sure the other woman expurgated a lot of them and toned down her basic dialect. Sometimes, though, when my sister and I would come panting in the back door from a long dusty game of Run Sheep Run through the orange orchards that lay between us and our neighbors, Rose would give us each a cup of water from the kitchen sink. "Let me do it, kids. You keep your crappy hands off my clean tap, you hear!" she'd say. And then she would snarl at us to stop that puking noise we bastards always made when we were thirsty. No doubt Mother knew about this lingo, but nobody bothered one way or another, and we learned to gulp politely, not like slurping little puppies.

Rose grew heavier as she stayed with us, and now and then Mother sent away to a mail-order house in New York that made extra-large dresses to buy what Anne and I thought were sumptuously giddy clothes for her. (Just as Mother herself grew fatter and perhaps longed to wear the kind of clothes she gave her servant, so she may have felt an unconscious envy for Rose's wild ugly past, so different from her own sheltered education in living.) The box would come by parcel post, and my sister and I would hurry out to the cabin under our big walnut tree, and Rose would try on the new dresses for us. It was a secret, warm moment. Anne and I would groan disapproval, or say yes, yes, *yes*. She would smooth the cloth over her firm, round body and look almost beautiful; then she would strip it off and fold it carefully back into its tissue paper for Billy to see on Sunday.

I don't remember if she ever actually wore any of the New York clothes. But neither do I remember how she looked with nothing on but her underpinnings: she dressed and undressed in front of Anne and me as casually as if we were her own children, or perhaps Billy. Once, Mother, who doubtless knew of our quasi-secret fashion shows in Rose's cabin, asked us if the blue silk fitted. We said, "Oh, yes—she's saving it for Billy to see," and Mother smiled a little.

Billy's gentling effect on Rose was one reason Sundays at the Ranch were special. Another was that, soon after we moved down Painter from the town and almost immediately after Grandmother died, Anne and I wrote a manifesto to our parents. In it we outlined our reasons for not wanting to attend Sunday school at St. Matthias. As potentially deft young politicians, we argued that Father should not have to interrupt his Sunday ranch jobs to drive us up to Whittier and then go again to bring us home and that Mother should not have to supervise getting us properly into our Sunday clothes and then out of them again, while Rose was occupied with Sunday noon dinner. We also touched on how much more useful we would be to everyone on the Ranch, doing countless small chores instead of learning for the *n*th time about Moses in the bulrushes.

We printed the manifesto, got Rose and the handyman, Little Ears, to sign as witnesses on two carefully dotted lines, and won our case with dispatch and to general rejoicing. As far as I ever knew, my parents felt serenely guiltless about depriving us of our weekly spiritual guidance, and Sundays were *free!* They were days of tranquillity and general bliss. Perhaps we slept later on rainy winter Sundays, but usually we got up early and eagerly. Breakfast was special, with waffles now and then, and no school, and no piano practice. We talked and laughed. The new batch of babies (Mother would have presented us with a fresh couple of siblings every eight years or so, if nature had permitted) splashed cereal and spilled milk happily, and Rose mopped up the table without scowling at them and hummed in the kitchen. Father would come to the breakfast table in his coverall instead of his usual office clothes (three-piece navy-blue serge, stiff white shirt, Sulka tie). The coverall was a huge, shapeless khaki jumpsuit that a garage mechanic had given him. Many years later, prime ministers and paratroopers made it stylish, but in about 1919 it was unlike anything we had ever seen—a mysteriously Sundayish garment that summed up our loose-limbed holiday enjoyment. He did not even button it at the throat, but Mother smiled at him as she dreamily untied the smallest baby's bib and pushed back the high chair.

Father puttered over the Ranch all morning, from his cramped little toolroom in the back of the barn. We tagged after him, never intruding on his Sunday reveries, awed by his concentration as he checked on when he had last mated his sole buck rabbit with one of the does, and how many eggs his pigeons were hatching into doomed squabs, and what his six hives of bees were doing with the three new queens he had bought. Sometimes he would put on his bee hat, oddly glamorous with its thick green veil, and pull on his special bee gloves, and climb up to the hives on the roof of the tractor shed. Anne and I would watch silently from under an avocado tree, but he seemed unaware of any of us as Rose called out to Mother, "There goes the Mister, up on that shaky old roof," and the other woman would stand silently in an upstairs window of the Ranch house. It was dramatic and tense. It was part of the special magic of Sundays. Now and then, angry bees would hum around Father when he lifted the lids of their hives, but he never was stung—more magic!

Sunday noon dinner was something we all thought about as soon as our voluptuous Sunday breakfast was over and Mother had stood up from the table. We dressed nicely for it, but not in churchgoing gear. Father wore a white shirt and a tie, but in summer no jacket. Mother now and then stuck into her topknot a flower Anne and I had picked for her, and we, too, had extra-clean fingernails and smooth hair. And the meal would be deli-cious, well served by strong, violent Rose. Mother always looked fine at her end of the table, serving the vegetables while Father stood to carve the roasted fowl or meat. Then there was a Sunday dessert—something special. We ate in contentment, politely and with controlled voracity.

We knew that we must sit down precisely at half past noon, because at twelve-fifteen Billy got off the bus at the corner of Painter and Whittier Boulevard, and since he and the bus were always on time, he was already in the backyard waiting for Rose to be free. Once he appeared, Rose leapt into action as if she had been lagging all week, ever since he last caught the night bus back to Los Angeles. She always did everything fiercely, but on Sundays she was almost ferocious, in an inspired and genuinely contented way, and she served us the good meal she had cooked with a special dexterity. We did not dawdle, but we ate with quick enjoyment, knowing that Billy waited outside while she did her dance around us and in and out the swinging door. We all felt happy. Oh, strawberries and little cupcakes; oh, fried rabbit! Fresh peas!

Father had hung a legless bench from the big walnut tree by Rose's cabin and had painted the old thing white. Sitting in it was a nice way to move back and forth in the dry air, and Anne and I loved it. We never climbed up onto the seat on Sundays, though, because it was Billy's then. Rose said to us, a few days after she came to the Ranch, "When Billy's here, you kids just leave him be. He's got things on his mind. He needs his rest." We would wave to him from the back porch as he sat in the swing, his short legs dangling just as ours did. He smiled at us, timidly, and once he brought a bag of hard toffee and gave it to us when Rose was not around; but he plainly liked to be by himself on the old bench swing until Rose was free for him—free from all of us.

Billy was a slender, shadowy man, with thin, graying hair and a remote face. It surprised Anne and me, as we peeked at him on Sunday mornings, that he could climb up into the swing so nimbly and keep it moving without touching the ground with his short legs. He was a pimp, I learned much later, but was planning to retire. He had been in the pen twice for something or other.

Billy loved waiting for Rose, swinging slowly back and forth until she signaled to him and he came silently into the kitchen to sit beside her, in the little corner ·called the breakfast nook, and eat her good food. Then they deftly and swiftly prepared the room for our Sunday night family foray, and they disappeared. They went out to her shabby quarters—slipshod housing that was considered fitting for hired help in those days, but at least it was private—and they spent the rest of the day together, making love and probably talking. They sent out a feeling, to Mother and Father and to us children, that they loved each other.

Sunday night supper was fun, with Rose not there to glare at us if we guzzled or slouched. Mother sometimes made oyster stew. At breakfast on Monday, with school starting again and Father deaf behind his morning papers, Rose would be scowling her fierce black scowl at us—but somewhat more gently than later in the week.

Then for a couple of Sundays in a row Billy did not come down from the bus stop, and Mondays were rough for us. Mother was cranky and withdrawn. Rose seemed to grow even heavier and thicker and snarled more foully in the kitchen. After we had sweated our way home from East Whittier School through the dusty orange and walnut groves, we steered clear of her and drank from the dogs' faucet in the backyard.

Rose asked for an extra day off, and went to Los Angeles, and never came back. She telephoned to Mother: Billy had been killed —knifed to death. She was already back in her old job on the street. Mother must send her stuff from the cabin to the Salvation Army.

It seemed impossible to Anne and me. Billy, kindly quiet shadow, would not come again on Sundays, to wait patiently in the old swing until Rose had taken care of us and then to love her alone in the little shack. We felt baffled. We missed Billy more intensely than we did her—for a while, anyway—and certainly more than we ever had our grandmother after her quiet disappearance.

Mother cried and ordered two new dresses from the New York catalogue and sent them to the address Rose had given her.

I doubt if they ever got to her, or if they were suitable to a way of life that my mother could only imagine but that she perhaps accepted for Rose in lieu of herself. And perhaps this was what the other Billy Sunday was shouting and pounding the Good Book about when Grandmother and I sat together in Bailey Street Park —hellfire and damnation, and all that.

—1982

17
The Jackstraws
(1922)

Every thinking man is prone, particularly as he grows older, to feel waves large or small of a kind of cosmic regret for what he let go past him. He wonders helplessly—knowing how futile it would be to feel any active passion—how he could have behaved as he did or let something or other happen without acknowledging it.

The only salve to this occasional wound, basically open until death, no matter how small and hidden—is to admit that there is potential strength in it: not only in recognizing it as such but in accepting the long far ripples of understanding and love that most probably spread out from its beginning.

A good time for me to contemplate such personal solutions, or whatever they may be, is when day slides into night. In almost all weather I can sit for a few minutes or an hour or so on my veranda, looking west-southwest and letting a visceral realization flow quietly through me of what other people have given me that I can only now understand.

A clear one, tonight, was of the jackstraws my Grandfather Kennedy whittled for my siblings and me in perhaps 1922 or before. It was never pointed out to me, as I now think it should have been, that an old man had spent long hours making something to please us. I blame my mother for this: she was constitutionally opposed to in-laws, and her whole attitude was that they must perforce be equally antagonistic toward her as the bride who robbed their roost of a fine cock and as a person of higher social station. This was unfortunate for all of us, and my mother lost the most by it and realized it much too late.

Meanwhile, whatever Grandfather Kennedy did was put into limbo in a subtly mocking way, and as far as I can remember we laughed a little at the clumsy set of jackstraws and pushed them into the back of the game closet, tempted by glossier packaged things like a new set of Parcheesi and even the baby stuff Tiddly-winks.

I still have a couple of the jackstraws. They are made of fine dry hardwood, and I think that some at the first had been stained faintly with green and red—dyes Grandmother may have brewed for her dotty husband, grinning sardonically as she prophesied in silence about the obvious end to the caper. One of the straws (were there a hundred in each set, with one hook to be passed around among the players?) is shaped like a crude mace. There were others like arrows, daggers. . . . Each one, according to its shape and then its color, was worth a certain number of points.

I cannot find the rules anywhere in my otherwise somewhat gamey shelves, but I know that the person chosen to be "first" held all the jackstraws firmly in his one or two fists, depending on his age and the length of his fingers, with the hook or perhaps the king straw in the middle, and then twisted them while everybody held his breath around the table. Then the hand or little fists let go, and the pile fell into a contrived heap on the table. And then —yes, the hook was kept out, apart, in order to start the trembling battle, and it *was* the king straw we'd left in the middle!—then we took turns and delicately plucked out one straw, then another if we had not jiggled anything, no straw at all if we had, always aiming for the main glorious one so deftly buried under the little heap. The hook was passed around. Whoever got out the prize won the game, and unless it was time for bed we had another game, drunk with the taste of deliberate skill and *kill:* after all, if you have dug down to that king straw and tweaked it out smilingly, you are yourself king—no matter what your sex—for at least twenty-three seconds!

This sounds competitive, a boring word to me. It is: competitive and therefore boring and probably to be frowned upon by now. But it is a game that was played very quietly, over and over, by men like my midwestern grandfather no matter what his age, and he handed it on to us. It was a silent game, except for occasional shudderings and little groans from the younger ones, quickly snubbed as weak. Grandfather sat like a giant prophet behind his silvery beard, which we knew in a completely disinterested way (at that age!) had been grown to hide his beauty from a horde of young ladyloves, and with an enormous bony brown hand he plucked one jackstraw and then, when his turn came around again, another from the wicked pile. We watched him like hypnotized chickens and tried to do likewise. If one of us missed, there may have been a quiet moan from the others but never a chuckle: we were taught not to *gloat* in public.

Outside the quiet house there was, as far as I remember, no sound, except toward morning an occasional coyote. Of course, there were wild rabbits and moles and mice, but we paid them no heed. Inside, the game was as intense as in any elegant casino, although that connection would have outraged Grandfather: he did not believe in gambling, yet he practiced it every night of his life with jackstraws, Parcheesi, and later crossword puzzles that he transposed into Latin. He would never say "bet," but he would say "wager"; he never said, "My little mare is twice as good as yours," but rather "She is better, I believe." His differences were semantic as well as religious.

So we picked delicately and passionately at the pile of whittled sticks, with their faint colorings, when we played in Grandfather's house. It was *quiet* there on his ranch near La Puente, in southern California. At ours, the game fell flat. He was not there. I see now that such was the reason, although then I thought, if I thought at all, that it was a silly *kid* thing, to be played patiently and politely with an old man. And as I now remember it, I barely thanked my grandfather for the set he had so carefully whittled for us. I had grown past all that. I was in another environment, another age in my own rapid transit from here to there. He was, in a way, stopped at what I hope was the enjoyment of sitting at a table in soft light and watching young people fix their eyes and lick their upper lips and control their fingers to pluck one nicely carved stick from underneath another, in order to edge toward the king itself.

I wish that I had told my grandfather then, in all the hurly-burly of Christmas when he presented the little box of jackstraws to us after such lengthy whittlings and colorings, that I realized what he had done. But I did not. I had no actual physical conception, much less a spiritual one, of what his gift meant. He was an old person and I was a young one. I knew nothing of patience, pain, all that. He could not possibly have tried to tell me about it. So he made a set of jackstraws, and here and now I wish to state that I finally know how to accept them. (At least, I *think* I do.)

It is too bad that my mother waited so long to slough off her conditioned reactions to being related by marriage to people who, in spite of everything she did, were better educated than her own parents but not as affluent. She held us away, willy-nilly, from much warmth, and knowledge, and all that. I don't blame her now. I simply regret it, as I do the fact that I cannot tell Grandfather Kennedy how much I love the two faded pieces of the jackstraw set that he made, and that we casually pushed aside, and that I still have.

—1987

18
Tally
(1923, 1928–1953)

No doubt there is a rich lode of written information about the invisible companions who sometimes walk beside us, or warm our chilly hearts, or wait timelessly to take our groping hands. Sometimes they have been called guardian angels and sung about and painted and made into statues and music. Probably students of the human mind and heart have made charts and lists and even diagrams of their appearance, of when and why they manifest themselves and to which human beings. Probably I should try to find out about all this, since surely records have been kept for our scientific if not spiritual edification. For I feel muddled, as I try to think about the reason why I slept for about twenty-five years with my hand hanging over the edge of any bed I lay in.

Until this night, perhaps a couple of hours ago, it had never occurred to me to wonder why I did this with such a warm feeling of trust and confidence, such an unquestioning surety that if ever the moment was right, my hand would be held in a strong warm other hand.

It is not a usual thing for a child to live with an invisible companion, but neither is it considered very rare, as far as I know. My brother David, who was eleven years younger than I, had a friend none of us ever saw, named Tally, and we seemed to take it for granted that although Tally was not visible to us, he was closer to David than any of us and was therefore our important friend. David and his sister Norah, two years older, were deeply attached to each other, more like twins than plain siblings, but I don't think Norah ever played with Tally, and I am not aware that she ever felt any jealousy. It is part of our general family acceptance, probably, that I have never thought to ask her.

When my next-younger sister Anne and I would come home from school and ask where were the kids, the little ones, Mother would say, "David's upstairs reading with Norah," or "Oh, he's been out all afternoon in the walnut tree with Tally." And on Sundays, when Father did not publish the *News* and we sat longer at table, he would ask David, "How's Tally these days?" David would say, "He's fine, I think. He cut his finger, though. It's all right." Then we would talk about other things, but not deliberately changing the subject. It was all very simple.

When David was perhaps eight, though, Father asked him one day at lunch how Tally was, and David said in a clear flat voice, not looking at any of us, "Tally has gone away." We did not speak for a minute, which may have been filled with shock or even horror. Mother made a little sound, finally, a kind of muffled *oh,* and Father said something like "That's too bad!" and we never mentioned Tally again, at least not to David and indeed almost never otherwise. It would have been rude or something like that.

As I think about all this, for the first time in perhaps half a century or even a thousand years, it seems improbable, but certainly the general acceptance of my little brother's companion was as real as everything else was then—as real as all our voices, and the smell of the old walnut tree, and the long dusty walks home from school, and the Sunday lunches. Now I wonder: Tally was invisible to us, but did David see him, as they played together for long fine hours? I remember that David read and talked aloud a lot to him and that he answered many questions that we never heard. It seems strange, now, that although Norah must have known more about Tally than any of us did, we never felt indiscreet enough to ask her what we knew we must not ask David.

And now I am trying to put into satisfactory words a description of another such visitor as Tally: the nameless, faceless, shapeless spirit who for about twenty-five years stayed under my bed, nearest to me while I slept.

Today a friend, whose left foot must feel wooden for a few months after a hardened artery was repaired, wrote that she was letting her leg dangle over the edge of the bed at midnight. It felt naked and silly, she said. And suddenly I was remembering about my companion, the ancient man who stayed so long nearby in case I needed reassurance. (Of course, I often did, but never enough to ask him for it, like putting off taking two aspirins in case you may need them more later than you do now.)

The person under my bed was a man, all right, and it seems strange that I never questioned or bothered about that nor about the fact that he was indeed somebody. I knew all this without any wondering at all, as a small child may understand without words or worry that someone loves and will care for him. The old man must have been tiny, because it did not matter if I slept on a real bed or on a pallet on bare boards: I simply let my left hand stay trustingly over the edge of whatever I lay on, even if I lay close to a dear lover or a sweet little child. And it did not matter if my hand hung sweaty in the tropics, or carefully escaping from heavy warmth in a snowland, or even from a high sterile hospital bed: I knew that when I most needed it, the old man there, tiny as a pea or big as a skinny child perhaps, would reach out and clasp it confidently in his own strong clean hand.

This comforter or friend or whatever he might be called was never named, at least by me, and indeed I seldom gave him a thought, consciously anyway. If anyone had asked me what he might look like, so faithful there beneath wherever I slept, I would have said something vague about tiny-bones-long-nose-wise-eyes-white-beard, perhaps. Mostly, I am sure, I would have got rid of the whole intrusiveness with a shrug and dismissing smile. I don't think I have ever told any human being about him, which as I write this now seems very odd. Certainly I was not embarrassed. It was simply that it seemed unnecessary, the way it was unnecessary to ask about what Tally did when he was with young David.

And now that I think about it, the strangest thing is that I do not remember when I stopped needing to put my left hand down over whatever I lay on, knowing that he would hold it if need be. (Once, I remember, I was lying on a bed of wild garlic in a Swiss forest!)

Certainly I need help now—or at least the assumption of its availability—as much as I ever did and perhaps more. But all I can do, at this stage in my life game, is feel very thankful that for a long time I knew that I was not alone. As I try to remember the hows and whys of this strange certainty, I feel truly puzzled about the whole silly business. All I know is that the tiny old man was there, if ever I needed anything more than my unspoken and largely unfelt belief that indeed he was. And I like to think that such presences, the kind that come and go without question or mockery or indeed even recognition, will stay near all of us. Tally was much more a part of my little brother David's life than my old man was of mine. He had a name, and perhaps, for David anyway, a recognizable image. My own guardian was nameless, unseen. But I knew that the firm grip of his hand would be there if ever I called silently for it, or even if *he* knew that it was time to take the hand I left out for him.

Sometimes now when I am between sleep and wakefulness, I wish that he were still down there, underneath the bed or the blades of grass between me and the earth. Once in a hospital I felt actively hurt, or at least baffled, that he was gone. Why had he left? I wondered irritably, half-amused at my childishness.

Well, it is plain that he is needed more somewhere else. I suppose David knew that about Tally, too, philosophically. And clinically, I doubt that my leaving my left hand free for a warm reassuring grasp from an invisible and nameless and formless presence was at all like spending long agreeable hours with a friend, as my brother did. My old man, who could be either bent into a bundle two feet tall under a real bedstead or tiny as a pea in the grass—but whose hand was always ready to hold mine—may not even have been one of the "invisible playmates" that child psychiatrists write books about. For one thing, I was too old: I think that I was about twenty when I first knew that he was there, all right. (That was in Dijon, under a high ancient French bed where I slept with my first husband. Need for any other comfort was not in my conscious mind, certainly, and yet that is when the little old man first took up his watch-and-wait station.)

As for his leaving me, I was not aware of it until a long time later (I've said twenty-five years, but it may have been much more) when I realized that I no longer put my hand outside the covers and down over the edge to tell him that I was there.

When did I stop? Speaking dispassionately, I would say that

I need his warm strong hand in mine more now than ever, but he is not there. My hand, left out, would grow cold and awkward. He is gone. But he and Tally are somewhere, of course, and that is good to know.

—1985

 19
Ridicklus
(1924)

I am thinking about the word *ridicklus,* not *ridiculous.* It's one of my private words, because of its ridiculosity, its complete silliness.

I think I began to use it when I was seventeen and in boarding school, first about Mrs. Brownley, our housemother. She was a dainty, extremely ladylike person, and she was ridicklus only because her first job at being a housemother was such a nasty tough one, for her at least: she had to spy on and then break up a ring of hard-core pornographic activity that went on for about two weeks, every night and often most of every night, after school started in the fall.

My younger sister Anne was one of the willing girls in a kind of cult or guild that had me a little worried about her, but never enough to tell her so. Of course, I knew all about it, but I was never a part of it. From what I remember of those toplofty years, I may have considered myself above it in some strange way, although all the people concerned with it trusted me and told me everything that went on. This may have been because I was so stupid or naive, but I really do believe that they trusted me because I would never have dreamed of telling on them.

The leader was a girl named Ivy, or Ina perhaps. She left the school in about a month and nobody ever missed her, although she was in complete control of the ring while she lived in the next room to ours. She was overtly in a change in her life when she became completely masculine. Of course, we were all like oysters at that age, so that we could go either way according to the tides and so on. My sister, for instance, was always very female and was disturbed by the maleness of Ivy/Ina, whereas I recognized the male-girl immediately and never thought any more about it. This recognition was tacit. No words were ever spoken between us, but Ivy/Ina knew that I did not worry about her, or myself, or even her partners in the hard-core porn cult and that my small worry about my sister was of no importance to anyone. I knew that Anne would survive it, and she did.

Ina/Ivy's roommate was a very feminine, exquisite little kid, very sexually aware and alert. It was said that she had been secretly married and had been separated from her lover by her irate and very rich parents and hidden in our prim and private boarding school. She was young, but only I knew about it all apparently, because she escaped one night through our bathroom window to her husband or lover and was never mentioned again.

While she and Ina/Ivy were together, they gave a little show late every night on how men and women made love, with Ina/Ivy always on top. I suspect that it was very primitive and simple "missionary" stuff. The girls, though, were even simpler, all of them, so this was an education in a way, and it could have been worse for them.

The night they were raided, I knew it was all arranged, and

by then I felt very sorry for Mrs. Brownley, and part of me wanted to warn her about it, but of course I did not. I did not warn the girls either. It went very quickly and discreetly, of course, and there was no talk at all on the surface, and the next night the little girl disappeared with her lover and then two weeks later Ina/Ivy went away, too, and my sister Anne went on in her own ways and Mrs. Brownley and I did, too, and I don't know who was left feeling the most ridicklus. To me, it was Mrs. Brownley herself, so impossibly ladylike was she and so ridicklusly impregnable was I. Or were we?

—1989

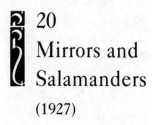

20
Mirrors and
Salamanders
(1927)

The fact that this visible, tangible world is only a hard and brittle reflection of the real existence in dreams has always seemed very clear to me. My sister Anne, too, knows that it is true and understands things that to many people seem unintelligible, preposterous, false. We both believe that to dream is to live—fully, completely. People say, "But when you dream you sit useless and staring, or lie like a corpse." It is true that when one dreams, one's body is useless, uninhabited—but how small a part of life is that weird machine called Body!

Several years ago I had the measles, and when I had recovered I told Anne and my friend Margie of my experiences. Among other things, I mentioned quite casually that one day I was a salamander. Margie snorted. I was silly, she thought, to say such things, because they were nothing but lies that might be heard by grown-up people. Why tell stories when I knew perfectly well that I had been

lying in bed most of the time, all speckled? I was delirious, probably.

Yes, I *was* delirious, but what was that but an easy way to be
—anything? This time I was a salamander. I could remember.

What? Margie sniffed.

Well, I remembered fire and jumping on my tiptoes from one
flame crest to the next. I knew that to fall into the hollow between
the flames would make me rather faint, because I was a very young
salamander. I was very small and lithe and beautiful in body, and
my hair was little bug wings. My eyes were pale green and flicker-
ing. Sometimes I ran across great stretches of ice.

That was a dream! vowed Margie. Of course, but I was the
dreamer, so why wasn't I the little salamander?

Well, how could I be one, when I was lying on the bed right
in plain sight? Anne demanded scornfully if Margie thought my
body was the only part of me, and I added that just because I
showed myself in a body to common people (meaning human
beings, I now suppose), it was no sign that I was chained to it and
obliged to wear it all the time.

Rather involved, you think, for small children to discuss? But
no! We were only putting into words what almost every child
knows, and what a few grown-up people remember and thank
God for: existence is not beef and steel, but beef and steel are
reflections in a crooked glass held before existence by—Adam and
Eve?

—Essay written at Miss Harker's School, Palo Alto,
May 6, 1927

21
Figures in a Private Landscape

I   Laguna, 1927: Journal

June 7

Several exciting things happened today.

Sis and Charles and I walked past Goff Island and back. We carried a lunch, laughed, shouted, leapt—three young fools. I love to spend a day like that—and end it hot from sunburn, tired as a dog, and very happy. A dog followed me all day: a lovely brown spaniel. Nothing flatters me more.

At about 4:00, E. Gilman came rushing in, sobbing that Dave had been gone since nine o'clock last night. Mother went right to their house. I was so worried—for D., but mostly for dear Mrs. Gilman. I could see him at the bottom of a cliff, kidnapped, arrested—but not running away, because he adores his mother. In an hour, she and Mother drove in—she white, haggard, but happy. He—the damned little brat—had driven up to Los Angeles to a show with two other young smart alecks and had spent the night at one of their houses! Oh, I could beat him. He just said, "Ah, what the heck! Don't you think I'm old enough to take care of myself? What the heck!" Mrs. Gilman told me that she had passed her high mark of worrying over Dave—if he is gone for a week or a month, she will never worry again as she did last night. He should be spanked—perhaps.

I notice in the paper that George Griffith is leaving next week for Liverpool, where he will live "on his own." I am so glad. He is probably going in order to study ships—and I think his parents are unusually gifted to see that he is made for that and nothing else. He will be doing what he is intended to do, thank God. It is reassuring to see something like that. He is young, not through high school, but very resourceful—a man of thirty in steadiness of purpose and dogged fineness. I like George.

Tonight I read *The Insidious Dr. Fu-Manchu.* I unconsciously see a red scorpion, an exploding fungus, under every cushion, and a yellow hand swaying the curtain. What a book! And isn't it queer that one part of me can be having the creepy horrors while most of the others are sane, quiet, amused?

My nose is red, Mother and Sis say. I asked Charles, and he remarked in a rather embarrassed way, "Well, it's not exactly flaming!" But I don't care—the trip down the beach was worth it, even if we didn't do what we set out for—explore the reef. Another time, that.

Mother mumbles, "Go to bed, Dotey." I will. It will be pure enjoyment.

July 2

One of the things Noni took to camp yesterday was her "line-a-day" book. She's been writing in it ever since May 30—most unusual in a child her age. I don't think I ever wrote for more than a month after January in all my attempts at keeping one. And how loathsome it is to read what I put down! I must have been a *very* objectionable child—especially during my first year in high school —so serious, so sad and drudging in my pursuit after things. I can still see myself, trying to look down my nose at popularity, and sex, and cheating—all in the same category, then. Now I realize that I *can't* look down my nose—perhaps because it turns up at the end. How I've grown!

But seriously, one reason I'm keeping this diary, as Mother insists on calling it, is because I *have* grown, in so many ways besides inches and vocabulary. I'd like to see if I have the mentality to write what I *want* to write—what I think. I doubt it. Damn it —what's my idea in forever playing to an invisible audience? Or not an audience so much as an observer? Sometimes, in those rare seconds of companionship that flicker between people I meet and me, I almost say what I want to, and then as I say the words in my mind, something utterly different comes out of my mouth and is twisted into a meaning I don't recognize—hate—sneer at. Well, I shall see—maybe—and this book will be amusing, even if it doesn't say what it's supposed to—maybe.

I felt as if a cannonball had plowed through me—painlessly, but leaving a clean, empty place—when Dave and Noni capered off with Mr. Downes. They were so excited. When we were driving down from home, Dave said, "There's a kind of half-laughing, half-crying feeling running up and down my back when I think of camp." I hope it stops at that. Noni looked beautiful—lovely clear mouth, chin, nose, and shimmering brown eyes. She's all the looks in the family, though Dave gets more comment. He's a male and has the same kind of body I have—not built for close inspection, especially from the shoulders up.

Last night Mother and I talked for hours, turning over and over in those uncomfortable beds, relics of our 1917 extra-poverty. We talked of marriage and men—her beaux; her family; mine;

marriage and other relations with Jews. This morning I dreamed I was engaged to a horrid little Jew—funny-paper type—and had to get his immigrant mother off the boat. I recognized her—a beautiful woman like Jo Isenstein's mother—and went up to her as she sat on a bench. I forgot my fiancé's name! I said, "Oh, you're Morrie's mother, aren't you?" and she said, "Not Morrie's." "Then you're Izzy's." "No, not Izzy's." "Sidney's, Levi's, Ben's?"

It was terrible because she was so calm, so dignified and benign, and I felt as if each horrid name I threw at her was an insult to her beautiful eyes. I don't know how it ended.

Mother has been heating a little water, and when I asked her what for, she said it was to wash some towels. Now I find her mopping the kitchen floor! Now why did she lie? I think it was because she knows I would offer to help her, and she wants to do that job—to pull, and moan, and flop onto the daybed with a long dying note like that of a balloon with a beautiful whistle—if there is such a thing. Tomorrow when Father and Sis and Helen and Norris and the kids and N. and I are all in one room, she will say, in that high, gay voice that sometimes is forced, "Well, I got down on my hands and knees and simply *scrubbed* the kitchen yesterday!" We will say, "Heavens!—*Why!*—Damn fool thing to do! —How terrible!" Then she will look at us in that seemingly deprecating way of hers: "Well, I *know* I shouldn't have done it, but it was perfectly *filthy*—*rotten* filthy—and it gnawed at me until I felt just as dirty! I finally decided there was nothing to do but clean it. Now look at me—stiff as a board—but it was worth it. 'S nothing I despise worse than a dirty kitchen!" We'll all grin inwardly— with her—and outwardly send out waves of appreciation of her love of cleanliness.

We may drive to the Gilmans' this afternoon. It will be nice to see Mrs. G. and the girls—it will be bothersome and sad to see

Dave. He is building his wall of henpecked shyness so fast that I simply haven't the energy to climb over, much as he wants me to. Poor boy.

Last night Mother and I went to the new café, Las Ondas, and I saw Don Brown with his family and a nice girl whose wool-covered ear he whispered into. He looked at me, long and seriously, from his sad eyes. I looked at him, ruminatively, I think. Then we both looked away and studied each other covertly until Mother and I left. Now why? Why do a stupid, lazy thing like that? Oh, hell, this is going to be a mixed-up summer, unless my feelings are all crooked. I wish Tony were here—he was so restful.

Yesterday, M. and I went to Van Altman's, and I picked out two presents which the kids will give me tomorrow, much to my surprise and delight. Darlings! I also bought a kind of yoke of Chinese embroidery—colors enchanting and outlines very arty. I may use it—probably not—but it is so satisfying!

July 12

I've just finished my sixth—or seventh—cup of coffee. Mother is in Whittier, putting up apricots, and Sis is at Dana Point with Carlos, so I seized the chance. I *love* coffee, and it gives a very delightful sensation to gulp down one more cup than I really want, knowing that M. and Sis would say, "Now, *Dotey!*" if they were here. I'm so full of coffee that if I jumped up and down I could feel it make little waves in me. That's amusing, in a way.

I feel very sad today. My eyes ache, my foot aches, my heart aches. Sis always reduces, or raises, relations with my friends to a sex basis. Perhaps she does it unconsciously—what does it matter? —but it simply spoils things for me. Last summer she broke up my perfect triumvirate, and now she has completely spoiled my feeling toward Carlos. She flatters him, teases him, irritates him, presses his hand—things I do, but in a very different way. He is bewildered—he knows that she has suddenly become interesting, in a new way. Damn it—I wish she'd leave him alone. He's just a little boy and, until she started, was my young brother. Until last night I have never needed to powder my nose—of course I have done it, but not to please him. Now he announces that he likes Anne's nose—probably the first time he's ever noticed a girl's feature in a masculine way. Oh, well—I've always known he'd grow up, but I'd looked forward to one more summer of companionship.

Saturday afternoon Sis and C. and I walked down to see the children and I suggested that he and I climb the big rock. The tide was high, and the only way to get to the top, on the waveside, was half-covered, but I knew we could do it, helping each other. I went first, because I've done it so often before, with Carlos right behind me. I was halfway up and with my fingers and toes well placed, when a rather large wave washed up the rock. I had a good grip and was wondering if C. was safe, while the wave was still on me, when I realized that the spray was spoiling things. It rained on me and pulled my scarf up and then down over my mouth and eyes. I seemed to be wrapped in horrible wet silk, clinging to my eyes, pulling them shut, filling my mouth and nostrils. I shook my head frantically and let go of the rock with one hand to pull the damned thing from my face. Before I could do it, I heard the second wave coming and swung my arm back to the rock. I couldn't find a crack or hole to fit my fingers into, and called out as well as I could to Carlos. The water poured over me—a bigger, heavier wave—as I swung around. My fingers slipped and slipped, until I could not feel the rough rock under them. I pressed with my shoulders, my knees, the soles of my feet, against the rock. Then the wave receded and casually, carelessly flipped the scarf from my face as it did so. I slid down the rock and dropped on all fours on the wet sand, numb with pressure on the rock, and fear, and sick with anxiety about Carlos. Why hadn't he answered me? I couldn't see him in the water. Oh, God, I thought, what shall I do? I raced around the dry end of the rock and saw him there, giggling at Sis's efforts to throw his knife in a straight line. They laughed when they saw me come dripping up the sand—my scarf slapping against my arms, my eyes full of salty water, and my freckles standing out. I was furious—furious! To think that I had risked my life —almost drowned—for some silly fun with this cackling little brat! I wanted to fly at him—spank him—ridicule him. Instead I let him wrap his towel around my foot and tried to get it just as bloody as I could. The hole was deep and I succeeded in making it look awful—like Caesar's toga. Carlos and Sis were really awfully sorry I'd hurt myself—and so was I.

Do I sound like a jealous, disappointed baby? God knows I'm disappointed—and in a purely selfish way, I think—but I don't believe I'm jealous.

July 14

I simply *must* find something to do! It is wicked to waste these perfect months—three of them—I, young, strong, brave, and the world rolling round and round. But what can I do? If I get a job, it means that Mother and Sis are tied to the house. I feel, too, that there would be a silent (or not silent) reproach continually dogging me—"How can you leave this comfort, and love, and thoughtfulness, to go out in the world? Is this gratitude? Here we have planned a wonderful summer for you, and you throw it in our faces!" I see the point. It's up to me.

I'm praying to God, or Something, that I will be able to

sidestep this college business. But only two more months! God, you'd better work fast. If I only had some definite purpose in starting out, for Italy, or Uruguay! I'm just a mumbler in life, as far as I can see. I do everything poorly—much worse than not doing it at all. The only thing I do well is see—mistakes, blunders —the why and wherefore—and my own clearest of all. Is that unusual in a nineteen-year-old?

July 23

A great deal has happened—in a way. Dave has been ill, quite ill at times and at other times almost well. He came down from camp a week ago, cross as the devil and swathed with wet, soppy compresses. Mrs. Downes, the headmistress, brought him and I hated her. As mother said, she looked and talked like a woman who loathes children.

Dave grew worse—turnings, and tossings, and a temperature at times very alarming. Dr. Day, a consumptive, pale-eyed Bostonian whom both Father and Mother liked immediately, finally decided that D. *didn't* have intestinal flu. He was afraid a little briar scratch on the back of his neck had become infected on the inside and was poisoning his system. He advised us to take Dave home to our own doctor, as we no doubt realized that he himself was not strong enough to undertake the treatment of any possible complications. He thought the child was physically strong and doubted that we would have any trouble, but—home was the best place. Here the sanitary conditions and—uh—well, good-bye, and please let me know how the dear child gets along.

That night, Monday, I telephoned to Helen, and the next morning she and Mother and Dave sailed off to Whittier, he leaning back, grinning quite sheepishly.

Sis and I followed, into awful heat. I felt quite ill and wondered if one could possibly have a sunstroke through an auto top. At home, we found Dave without fever and still cross. Dr. Wilson, confident that the gland under the scratch was infected, had him firmly and wetly bound with compresses. Poor Dave! He longed for some fit mode of expression.

I perspired and squeezed orange juice. The next day Sis and I drove back and had fun wandering all over this end of two counties. Mother always keeps us on the beaten track, even in the way of eating places, so we exercised our comparative freeness by eating ham sandwiches at some little dump by the roadside. I went so far as to try to drink a bottle of near beer (why can't it be neer beer, or near bear?). I found that the teaspoonsful I stole from Father's glass were more enticing.

It was late when we reached the cottage, and the change from Whittier heat to Laguna coldness made us shiver, so we had a cocoa orgy. In the middle of it Mrs. Gilman came in, with a distraught look in her queer eyes. We lied beautifully about having finished our supper, and after the usual preliminary remarks, we found that she was very worried about Dave. He was picking peaches in Ontario—it was 107 degrees there—he was so careless about shaving every day—he always had nosebleeds when it was hot—he would forget to wear clean trousers—he was a careless driver—would one of us (of course she meant me) drive up with her to see if he was all right? But our plans were dependent on what Mother said over the phone the next morning—we might have to go up and get her and our Dave. Yes, that was so. Had we noticed the movie set on Goff Island?

The next morning she came at nine o'clock, and I naked. She *must* go to Ontario. I put on some clothes, phoned Mother and found Dave was worse, and started out with the poor woman.

The heat!—it was horrible to come out of this cool clearness into such pressing, choking heat! The perspiration ran down my arms into my hands, down my temples into my ears, down my cheeks. Mrs. Gilman talked about sun worshipers, love, Dave, and at Santa Ana stopped to buy a volume of Edna St. Vincent Millay. She couldn't find one. We ate a salad and an ice at some place where the seat was so hot it made me feel like a Japanese housewife or a South Sea priest. We went on like a fast wind to Ontario. I sat in a wicker chair under an apricot tree. Oh, my head! It was an ache that reminded me of my last week at Bishop's. I watched the sunlight in the poplars and looked at a big book of Thévenet's drawings. It slowly drew cooler. Dave came home, bellowing songs —loud and crude and abrupt as ever but tantalizing me with that ever-present hint of something better. I am always on the edge of something with him, and was never nearer than that night on the rickety pier—last summer. I think he hates his face and loves mine —and that night was very dark.

We came home that night, and the next morning when I phoned Mamacita, I told her that Dave went to sleep at the wheel and I drove. She said very calmly, "The hound!" She hates him for that awful day he didn't come home.

Our Dave had ear trouble. *That* was it! I felt like shouting, Hurrah! Hurrah! At last we knew. My darling little brother—my poor little brother—no more compresses for him! Of course, ears are worse, especially when they must be lanced, as his were, but to know! Aha! And he is much better, or was when I last talked with M. Tomorrow, if they—M., Dave, and Father—are not here by noon—that will mean he is worse! I can't think of it.

Yesterday I saw Noni—for the first time in almost a week. She is so beautiful. I love her. She was simply vibrating with ec-stasy over a letter Father sent her. She had asked him for an accordion, but told me with shining eyes that she would rather have that letter than even *fifty* of the best accordions in the world. I know what she means and feels.

Bill, the lifeguard at the camp, has finally dared to talk to me, after three weeks of admiring and rather appraising glances. I am afraid he is something of a scrub—in more ways than in being shorter than I. I imagine that with a little encouragement—but shall I give it? Who knows—who cares? I hate his mustache.

Thinking of the other kind—Bob Cowling may come down with "Cholly" Greene tonight. I wonder if he'll even see me this time. I don't believe he's the type that will be embarrassed by last year's innocent interlude. Of course, I can't tell, because I don't know him. He's very apparent, however.

Just for the amusement, I hope I attract him again. This thing of swearing off the company of both kinds of the species has its dull side. And I want to dance tonight.

The Chinese blue-green bowl is full of shining plums, and some have rolled onto the maize linen napkin. It is unattempted and delightful, but the combination is disturbing, too.

Aunt Maggie has inspected the suggested room and finds it unpleasant. She wants Mother and me to go to Los Angeles with her and look at other living places. Oh, *who* has seduced my fairy godmother? I'm sure I have one, someplace. Only she and Circumstance can keep me from college, for a definite stand on my part —really the only solution—would hurt Father and Mother to their hearts' cores. No, it's college for me.

August 27

And how very disgusting that I'm too lazy to keep a promise— even one made to myself! I swore that I'd write in this stupid book at least once a week—even under difficulties. I have had those. Right this minute I can hardly write: I am sitting on the very edge of a couch which is at least two feet farther from the desk than it should be. I think that I'll slide off in a minute. I am in Mr. Altman's shop now. I've been working for him, in the afternoons, for about three weeks, and he has just left for San Francisco, leaving me in complete charge. Sis is helping me make change and so forth. Thank God he's put the dripping fountain and the green vase and the coats in the bank. I'd be worried about them. I like to work here, and besides earning $2.00 a day, I have learned more than I thought possible about Chinese art, and customs, and beliefs. It has been worthwhile in other ways, too: I've learned more about people, myself, my feet. I have more sympathy for salesgirls who have to stand up all day. Of course, I don't, but it sometimes seems so.

Astounding! I am going to Illinois College—have escaped the Ranch! Hurrah! Half an hour after Uncle Walter arrived with the announcement that Nan is going there this winter, we decided, telegraphed, arranged, talked, and carefully avoided the fact that I will be gone nine months—and for Christmas! It will be the first of many times, I suppose.

From what I can gather, the college is small—five hundred—coeducational Presbyterian, cold, old, famous for debates and sports, and loads of fun if you can avoid the YWCA and like splendid groups. I will.

Mother and Father have bought me a gorgeous fur coat—pony and beaver—and of course I have a lot of lovely new clothes, so I feel very well dressed.

I'm going east with Uncle Evans, which will be much more fun than by myself. I'll probably spend most of Christmas vacation with him, and the rest with Uncle Walter's family. Easter vacation I'll go to Aunt Ab's—I *hope.* I'm really scared to see her, because

I'm afraid my eight years' old memory of her will spoil the reality
—or vice versa.

Yes, this year will be amusing, and *much* better than nine
months in a boardinghouse. *Every*one congratulates me on not
going to the Ranch—everyone except Ernesta Lopez. She's disappointed, sincerely, which is a true compliment.

For Saturday, the shop is very dull. I wish people would flock
here while Alty's gone, so he could congratulate me when he
comes back.

Yesterday Sis and I went to see Margaret Leslie, who is working for Florence Barnes. People say that her family is furious at her
for working as a "common" maid, but we admire her immensely.
As she says, she'll need money at Mills this year (she's won a
scholarship there), and she does nothing but waste her time at
home. More power to her! She's a very charming girl. I hope she
and Sis see each other this winter. I told her about Betty Hull,
who's going there, too—both nice girls, well meaning, subtle as
brickbats, and good students.

Just finished reading a letter from Eda. She annoys me intensely, stirs me a little—too much for comfort—and fills me with
rather amused pity. She asks me to go to the University of London
with her, in 1928. It would be a glorious adventure—with almost
anyone else—Sis, perhaps.

I hope Sis never knows how much I love her. This year rings
like a knell in my soul—when I let it. I feel as if I'll never be with
her again. Last night she said that we'd have to have separate
Christmas cards this year. True—but my heart turned on its side.
Our trips to Samoa, to Somalia, to France—our bicycle tour
through Ireland—where will they be in ten years? With other
dreams dreamed well?

Grandmother and Grandfather came down yesterday, laden
with zinnias, and eggs, and peaches. They look . . .

September 4

. . . I suppose I was going to say—They look very fragile. But why not? They've lived long, and strenuously, and hard. I'm fond of them both, but I think I really love him the most—she's irritating.

The summer's over—done—finished. I feel filled with tears, and longings, and very vain regrets. How criminal it is to waste three months—but were they wasted? Assuredly, I did nothing I had planned to do, but I did other things—worked for Alty, made six hats and a negligee, thought a little, talked a great deal—and so on.

I don't think I made any friends—in fact, I may have lost some. I grew to like Hannah much more, and Elizabeth less, and they me in the same order. Louis has liked me, judging from his letters, more and more, and I him, but not in a heart way at all—on my part, that is. I was lazy this summer—didn't go out for men and therefore not with them either. I can say, as can almost any girl, no matter how ugly or how good-looking, that I didn't have the usual men around me simply because it was boring to attract them. That is sincere.

But for the sake of the gaiety of nations, I hope that this winter I won't be so damn lazy and particular. I hope the Illinois men are more interesting than this summer's crop of Lagunatics—and better looking. And while I'm damning, I'll damn Tony Lowett. He completely ruined the mental and physical appearance of any man I've ever met since. Of course, he couldn't help it—poor dear.

I have on a very attractive new black crepe de chine and my new black patent-leather oxfords from Paris. I feel very swagger—even with no one to look at me.

Sis and I've been taking roll after roll of pictures. I hope one of her and each of the kids is good enough to enlarge for my new pigskin frame. A horrible, sick fullness is always behind me, ready to slip into me whenever I dare think of going away. This is the fourth summer's end. I've felt it, but never so strongly. To leave Sis for nine months! And the family!

The house is charming—new paper on the walls—shiny floors—bright paint. Mother delights in it.

Last night Noni and Sis and I drove up in the closed car, and Dave came with Pete. Oh, it was so blissful to take a hot bath! Next summer, thank God, we're going to have a tub and a heater at Laguna.

September 6

A rather eventful day—Father went to a luncheon of the cast of *Gentlemen Prefer Blondes* and sat with Charlotte Treadway, the leading lady. She wrote a message to me on his menu—Mary Frances, Just oceans of health, happiness, and success—Charlotte Treadway. Aha! She almost sent word that she'd be glad to hear from me. We're all going to the opening night of the play, as a last windup, and I may meet her.

A very fervent letter from Louis—special delivery—announces that he is coming to say good-bye. He asks for several dates—in my last week at home! He'll be down Thursday, I think. We'll take him to *Gentlemen*. I'll be very glad to see him—but I do wish he could have come earlier. However, he's a dear boy—very dear.

Bob Ridgeway called tonight and, after talking for what seemed hours, asked me to go to the show tomorrow night. He's a pathetic person. I think I like him—and I'm afraid he's a little off about me. It won't hurt him—but I hate to have him spend his hard-earned salary on a person who cares so little for him.

Today I got two very kind letters—one from the head of the YWCA at I.C. and the other from my "big sister," who says she is "almost five feet tall." Oh, dear, oh, dear.

Joy and Carlos are coming over for luncheon tomorrow. Oh, dear. They are darlings.

September 8

Carlos was terribly shy and bored—held my hand a long time when he said good-bye and kissed his hand to me. Poor kid! Joy is as nice as ever.

Bob Ridgeway took me to see a very amusing comedy at the Playhouse, and then we went to Coffee Dan's. It's an interesting hole—supposed to be in a sewer, of course. The crowd was largely Jewish—pugilists and vaudeville actors—and the host is a very entertaining young Jew who introduces everyone to anyone and sings and so forth. We had to leave too early. I wished that I was with someone else. Bob is so awfully serious.

This has been a quiet day. This morning Sis had her gland removed. Poor kid—it wasn't pleasant, but she's very brave. I tried to make a hat this afternoon, and narrowly escaped apoplexy.

Tonight we went to the Ranch to bring the children, who've been spending two days there, back to home and Mother. It meant saying good-bye to Grandfather and Grandmother—perhaps forever. She said, "Good-bye, my dear. We'll try to be right here when you get back." Oh, hell.

Louis just called up from Pasadena. The same soft, slow voice and amusing laugh—but idioto! Why doesn't he come before tomorrow night? He hasn't so much time to diddle-daddle. He's so damned ponderous—but I do like him.

I'm *cross*. I'd better stop.

I am at Illinois College, in Jacksonville, Illinois. Several interesting things have happened since I left home, ten days ago, but I'm too cold to write about them—and until day before yesterday I was too hot.

Uncle Evans and I had a very quiet trip—so hot the last two days that we panted. Bernard met us in Chicago, and we did all kinds of things solely for my amusement. (I was too hot to appreciate them, however, until later.) We rode on a bus top out to the lakefront, went to the top of the Tribune Building, ate in the Grillroom of the Bismarck, and went to the stock exchange. I saw a horse faint, which impressed me a great deal. Chicago seems dirty. The women don't wear as much makeup as those in Los Angeles do, and their skirts are shorter. I didn't notice the men, except in the stock exchange, where they looked hard, keen, and very nervous, for the most part.

The trip down was awful—long and hot and sooty—and my first impression of Academy Hall worse. I can't describe it, now, anyway.

I must stop.

This thing is mostly starts and stops—but then, what isn't?

Things grow better. My frame of mind is very queer; I can't analyze it. I am lonesome, uncomfortable, full of longing for my family and decent climate and surroundings—and yet so interested in these people, their looks, conversation, habits, everything, that I would hate to leave. That may be my ultimate degree of contentment—who knows? I feel, too, that to admit defeat this third time would simply prove to Father and Mother that I am a coward for life.

Aunt Tim sent my curtains yesterday, and they make my room look twice as nice as it did. They are printed linen—orange and black and green and so forth in a very "modern" design. My floor lamp is orange. I hope Mother sends my India bedspread. I want to put it on the wall. Then with one or two more pictures and my Chinese pieces, it won't be a bad alcove.

Tonight is a wet, cool one. The streets look like patent leather.

This afternoon Nan and Rachel, her roommate, and I walked downtown and bought a lot of little things—pins, thread, grapes, and so on. It was fun, in a kind of detached way. That is how everything seems and has seemed ever since last spring. I feel as if I were swinging between two groups of existence—as if I needed some awful shock to bring me into reality again. I dread that, but this living without realizing it is futile, it seems to me. I *want* to do things intensively.

Nan is an awfully sweet little thing, and I'm very glad I've come here, for I'd never have known her in any other way. I hope she gets into Stanford next year, but I'm afraid she's definitely decided on Chicago. And I've definitely decided on Cal—though I *can't* think of cheering a team against Stanford. But I *must* be near Sis next year—maybe, if she's at the Good Samaritan, I'll go to the Ranch! How amusing.

—*1927*

II   Uncle Evans

(1927)

Uncle Evans was my mother's favorite brother and perhaps my father's favorite man friend, and he was my favorite relative because he was worthy of all this family worship. He liked us, too, and spent many of his sabbaticals near us, writing unread law books. When I was eighteen he suggested, to my astonishment, that we travel together from California to Chicago, where he would go on eastward to his university post and I would go south to a small college. I now believe that he did this on purpose, to help me into new worlds.

It was my first train trip of more than three hours. I was dazed at escaping the family nest. My clothes were correctly navy-blue *crepe de chine* (because of the soot), and I slept in the upper berth because I was younger than my uncle. I spent most of my time on the observation platform or in the ladies' room washing my hands. We met for lunch and dinner.

Uncle Evans was a seasoned commuter between West and East from the turn of the century until about 1940. He even had special clothes made for those gritty but delicious "trips," as they were always called: odd-looking three-piece suits made of "dirt-proof" alpaca or something. (Only white shirts, of course, with starched collars: he was a *professor*.) The trains were good. He knew them. He knew the conductors and porters and dining stewards. He even knew the engineer.

In those days (1927 for my maiden voyage), the trains stopped often, and there were still a few Harvey Houses along the line. ("The only test of a good breakfast place is its baked apple," Uncle Evans said mildly. "The Harvey girls never fail me.") One time Uncle Evans walked me up to the engine at a desolate stop, and we stayed too long and were hauled up bodily into the cab until the next slowdown. It was exciting. And there were still prairie-dog huts along the track and conelike ovens in the westward country, in silent ugly Americanized villages that still dared not tell the Indians what kind of bread to bake.

As an old hand, Uncle Evans knew where to ask the dining-car steward to put on things like live trout, venison, fresh corn, melons. They were served to him at our twinkling, snowy little table in the restaurant car, at noon and at night, and I paddled along happily in the small sensual spree my uncle always made of his routine travelings. I probably heard and felt and tasted more than either of us could be aware of.

One time when he looked at me over his menu and asked me whether I would like something like a fresh mushroom omelet or one with wild asparagus, and I mumbled in my shy ignorance that I really did not care, he put down the big information sheet and for one of the few times in my life with him, he spoke a little sharply. He said, "You should never say that again, dear girl. It is stupid, which you are not. It implies that the attentions of your host are basically wasted on you. So make up your mind, before you open your mouth. Let him believe, even if it is a lie, that you would infinitely prefer the exotic wild asparagus to the banal mushrooms, or vice versa. Let him feel that it matters to you . . . and even that *he* does!

"All this," my uncle added gently, "may someday teach you about the art of seduction, as well as the more important art of knowing yourself." Then he turned to the waiter and ordered two wild asparagus omelets. I wanted for a minute, I still remember, to leave the dining car and weep a little in the sooty ladies' room, but instead I stayed there and suddenly felt more secure and much wiser—always a heady experience but especially so at nineteen. And I don't believe that since then I have ever said, "I don't care," when I am offered a choice of any kind of food and drink. As Uncle Evans pointed out to me, I either care or I'm a dolt, and dolts should not consort with caring people.

—1945

III Examination Books:
Biology 9

(1927–1928)

I

To state and define the characteristics of protoplasm is a thing I should know how to do. Once I did know how—two or three months ago, perhaps. Now, in the final examination, I do not know—and I do not care. I am losing five hours of credit. Too bad, isn't it?

I broke the promise I made to myself, to let my so-called diary go for a year without reading it, and read it yesterday. I found it most interesting. I think it would bore and perhaps disgust anyone else—but it isn't meant for anyone else. It lacks unity, but so do I, at times. That sounds silly, because I suppose it's impossible.

II

This year has been an amazing adventure in many ways. I've been interested, but thank God I'm ending this part of it tomorrow. My train leaves for dear old California at noon—and I'm going to do nothing but read, and eat, and sleep, and look at the country. It seems to me that that's what I've been doing for five months. I've been lazy, scholastically. There's been no incentive to learn—and I've missed so much that it was impossible to make up botany—impossible if I wanted to pass my other subjects, which I did. I think that I'll emerge with about ten and a half of the sixteen hours I've been working for.

I feel sometimes as if I'd spent most of my time either on the train or in the hospital. Of course, that's exaggerated—only four trips across the country and two weeks at Passavant—but it's too much.

I hate like hell to leave Nan—but it's a good thing, I think. The newness of our very true friendship toward each other is wearing off, of course, and I'd rather say good-bye before we irritate ourselves. She's a fascinating person—I love to look at her —her Brenda-like face, her youngly voluptuous lines. She is very intelligent.

Rachel I hate to leave, too. She is comforting—like a great warm woman who smells cinnamony and feels soft—like a tender-eyed bitch. She gets on my nerves, though—just occasionally. I hope I see her again sometime.

We three have had a lot of fun this year. I've spent most of my time in their room—mine was so hideously colored and so empty of humanity. (The dainty, proper librarian had it last year and seemed to leave no feel of occupation, as most people do. And I don't think of the girls who have lived in it before—they were probably like the girls who go to Illinois College now, unalterably boring.)

III

We've been poor, and rich, and just moderately both—and have spent all our money on silly things: movies, and hot chocolate, and *food*. Ye gods! We must have bought twenty-five packages of cream cheese, quarts of ginger ale, hundreds of crackers, a whole garden of lettuce, barrelsful of jam. It was fun to eat the pale green leaves, and the richly colored jam, and the suave cheese, and drink the exciting ginger ale—on a candlelit table, with the Victrola moaning blues in the corner of the room. Sometimes Rachel and Nancy sang, and I lay on the bed, watching the light on their hair and their soft young throats. Sometimes we went to a movie, and sat in the balcony, with all the little boys, and laughed and clapped uproariously with almost no excuse.

Sometimes we went to the College Boys' Café, where we ate

waffles and vegetable soup and more waffles, and drank coffee, and once ate an awful apple dumpling. Usually Nan and I went together. We laughed at nothing—and Rachel isn't much good at that, tho' she's learned to do it more easily than she did in September.

IV

Once I gave a party. We all went to the C.B.C. and ate a ghastly meal with great gusto and then went to *Seventh Heaven,* presented by a very poor stock company. Funny things happened to us—I smile now when I think of them, and I shouldn't, because the botany assistant might notice it and come to see how I'm getting along with my examination. That would be embarrassing.

I've met some interesting people this year—Nan, Rachel, Mr. Anderson, Mr. Smith, Miss Elly, Miss Moore, and Miss McCune —these are the most interesting. Of course, I like the Rammelkamps, and some of the boys I've had dates with, and Sally Carter —and maybe I won't forget them as soon as I think.

It's queer about Mr. Smith and Miss Elly. I've seen him often —every time I've gone to history—but I've spoken to him perhaps four times. He's fascinating—not as a man to me, but as the epitome of brave looking in the face of awful odds, as the spirit of careless adventure. His lectures are thrilling. He has a dramatic instinct or urge—and when he tells how Marie Antoinette teetered into the Estates-General, how old Uecker drove through his report, how flaming Mirabeau pulled at the emotions of the representatives—I feel faint with excitement. I think I shall read much history.

As for the poor Miss Elly—I met her one night eating her thin little sandwiches wrapped in lace napkins and drinking her peptonized milk from a silver thermos bottle—sitting in the huge, dark, gaunt dining room that she once laughed and flirted in. Once she had lived there, in that shadowy house that the Art Institute has got and is using—and now, when her companion is "taking her day out," Miss Elly brings her supper and sits all alone at the long black table in the dining room. The electric bulbs, naked and dusty, send awful glaring light down on her mottled, diamond-heavy hands and on her thin silver hairs. The only sound is that of her chewing, or perhaps rats skittering through the great dim rooms upstairs.

That night she talked to us almost constantly. At first we were secretly cross—our nice picnic with Miss Moore and Miss Mc-Cune spoiled by a garrulous old lady. Then we realized her proud loveliness, her need to tell us of this room, this house, fifty years ago—of the mistress with her stiff brown side-curls, the carriages, the traveling farmhands, the butler house with its cold twinkling stream—on and on, in a fascinating stream of sometimes almost incoherent chatter. When we said good-bye, she said, "I want you girls to come see me. I'd *like* to have you call on me. You'll come? Now, young Harry Capps—he's a nice boy—lives right next to me. Ha—*that*'ll bring you!"

I wish I could write about Miss Elly—poor little Miss Elly.

Miss Moore and Miss McCune and their beautiful old house and their delicious things to eat, I shall never forget. I must write to them, because I feel much affection for their gentle charm, and I think they are fond of me.

I've really done lots of exciting things this year—the weekend in Chicago with Tim and Walter and Nan—my trips with Uncle Evans, the weekend with the Ridgestones, my trip to Bloomington with Ed Cleary—oh, many things. I know that when I go home I won't do as many things and won't have as many dates, but other things will make up for it. I'll have my lovely room, and my own bathroom, and good food, and clean air and warmth, and no more

pains in my chest—and books and concerts and plays, God willing. And Dave and Noni! I love them, love them.

Such things as checking trunks and so on bother me, but I
know that God protects fools. Tonight will be amusing, as I'll have
to sleep under a pile of coats—perhaps under a rug—all my blan-
kets will be packed. Nancy goes at eight o'clock, so Rachel and I
will hold the fort. She goes tomorrow night. I think she'll come
back—she's conscientious. I think she should, too, but not to that
awful hall.

Thank God this will be my last day of skidding on icy walks
and looking at mangy, sooty snow—for years, I hope. If I leave
California to live, I want to go in other directions from this country
—to the South Seas, maybe, or perhaps Alaska, because there the
snow is entire and white.

How queer to think that I am going—going as unexpectedly
and with as little cause as I came, leaving a few marks of myself
which will soon rub out or remain faint smudges—taking a few
permanent lines on my own—what should I say? blackboard? I
took much more of Jacksonville than I gave or than it took from
me. That is as it should be, perhaps.

Now what am I going into? I am glad that I do not know.
Whatever it is, it will be interesting—to me, at least.

—Illinois College, Jacksonville, Ill.,
January 30, 1928

IV Oxy

(1928–1934)

When it was first suggested that I try to write something for *The
Occidental,* I was scared. My mind was full of things I often say to
myself about my two short but deep experiences in the college,

but it seemed impossible to me to sort them into the neat little sections that such an imposing assignment should have. How could anyone possibly care about a sophomore in 1928 who tried so hard to get a Gertrude Lawrence tan that she almost knocked herself out several times on the hot bright roof of Erdman Hall? And why would it matter to anyone but perhaps a few ghosts that several years later the same foolish female found herself a faculty wife, chaperoning dances and trying to look at least twice twenty-five years old?

I even asked a couple of current college celebrities about my fumbling need to put nostalgia into focus and to find one salient thing to write about instead of several dozen, and they both murmured comforting advice that flowed past me with futile speed. One told me soothingly to close my eyes and let images come and go. Another asked me, much like a kindly priest or doctor, what I felt as a ripe old graduate about being able to remember landmarks (like Oxy, of course!) in most of my seventy-eight years hereabouts.

I felt impatient but did as they suggested. My theory is that when outside help has been asked for, one should either put up or shut up, and as the free-flow images surged past me and the landmarks grew and then shrunk and grew again, I doggedly sorted and agreed and rejected. It was fun, especially since I learned more about my two advisers than they would ever guess and met my own self on a few new planes. Finally, without author qualms, I decided to try to state why I feel strangely proud and fine about belonging willy-nilly to the Fifty-Year Club of Occidental College.

Now and then I recognize almost frantically that I was a lazy bum, which is always uncomfortable while it lasts. I knew that I was waiting for something to happen, and meanwhile I consented with innate dignity to live in a delightful little apartment in Erdman with my younger sister Anne Kennedy and even to join a sorority and, of course, go dancing as often as possible. And I worked hard on my tan. . . .

Dr. Ben Stelter was my best teacher. I admired him in a shy awed way and still do. He was the only one I really worked for. I was not brilliant, but I was fairly bright, and because I had gone to a couple of very tough prep schools, I did not have to turn more than a hair now and then to breeze through exams. I drew well and helped two or three people cheat on their papers in botany, without any qualms that I remember. I worked on the newspaper, second semester.

Anne and I had plenty of people to make our lives interesting. Her best girlfriend was Fay Shoemaker. I was less inclined to have one special person in my smug self-centered life, but probably enjoyed Helen Betts the most of the several attractive young females available. And I probably saw more of Count Jones than of any of the other men, because he was such a good dancer. I was not really interested in "dating" because I had an off-campus romance well into gear with Alfred Fisher, whom I married as soon as possible (in September 1929).

Larry Powell, a senior then, was the campus hero as far as I can remember: an irresistible little fellow, always in hot water but magically immune from open disgrace, who played politics and the piano with equal irreligious wizardry. Of course, I was too much in awe of him to do more than smile timidly when he began to date Fay Shoemaker (a freshman!), but soon after I left college, he joined my husband Al Fisher and me in France, and we all began a lifelong friendship, which included Ward Richie and Jim the Dutchman Gruenewegen and Gordon Newell, graduates from Occidental just before I went there.

Remsen and Helen Bird were in the president's house when I was first at Oxy and then about six years later, when he actually invented a job for Al Fisher as assistant to Dr. Stelter in the English

Department. Of course, I was in correctly respectful fear and trembling of the Birds when I was an undergraduate, but gradually as I peeked at Helen Bird sitting circumspectly in the curve of the piano at faculty wives' meetings, I permitted myself to feel a presumptuous fondness growing in me for both of them. Later we got over all the student–faculty-wife thing and became friends and even wrote letters, and they were as kind and amusing and subtle as any people I have ever known. The last time I saw them, they were walking down Geary Street in San Francisco, hatless and gloveless and laughing, and my two young daughters and I were walking up Geary, hatless, gloveless, laughing, and we hurried together just across from the two big theaters and embraced happily.

I wish that could have happened with Dr. Cleland. He was a warm fine person, too, but when I was a student I was much too shy to do more than tremble politely in his presence, and later I knew him only through other less mute admirers and, of course, what I read about him and by him. And there was a young bright man named Coones who carried on Dr. Cleland's work and whose wife I liked (still mutely) at our genteel afternoon meetings around Helen Bird's piano.

(The gray knitting that Helen always worked on in the crook of the big instrument was a trick, she told me later: she never had to say much, because she always seemed to be counting stitches. She would look up with a puzzled faraway smile if anyone asked her a direct question, and smile graciously again as one of her prestigious husband's henchmen's spouses would apologize for disturbing her, and then go back demurely to the gray pile in her lap. And after each meeting she would pull out whatever she had done that afternoon, so that several years later I spotted the same old knitting spilling out of its big straw bag by her bedroom door, waiting for another appearance with the president's wife! At least she never said it was for the missionary box, which I had been taught to do when I first picked up my knitting needles at the age of six or so and started to work on a gray woolen scarf for the poor freezing Alaskans—or was it for the poor naked Zulus?)

When Remsen Bird finally created a little job for Al Fisher, after we had got him safely into his *Docteur és Lettres* robes in Dijon and had spent the next three years sitting out the Depression on $45 a month in Laguna Beach, it was fun to swing into the mad social life at Occidental!

Al and I were almost suspiciously popular as chaperons, and the older professors encouraged us for obviously logical reasons connected with complete boredom. Of course, I loved getting a chance to whirl around the dance floor now and then with a senior or even a middle-aged teacher, after several years as the devoted wife of a nondancer. And it was fun to have to wear old-but-still-good clothes and even a hat now and then to a very respectable club or restaurant. And once, in the college gym, Count Jones himself turned up, and for a few minutes I was about nineteen again (in Scott Fitzgerald's first novel, written when he was about that age, he spoke very seriously of someone who was "a faded but still lovely woman of twenty-seven," which was about where I was, chronologically!), and the tall big-nosed fellow forgot that he was embittered by failing to pass his medical exams as his pal Bob Freeman had done so easily, and we pranced with incredible grace around the old gym. We were Ginger and Fred, Scott and Zelda . . . until I caught my dear husband's cold astonished glare.

And what was it about these separate and strange years that make me glad now that I am a member of the Fifty-Year Club? Can anyone really tell me? Was I learning how to be a thinking adult while I acted like a blandly unthinking child? Why did I not take classes and people and even *things* more seriously?

Actually, I believe that I am basically a serious person, and by now, more than fifty years later, I feel ashamed of a careless *acceptance* of all the easy good things, as if I had earned the right to them! I concentrated on tanning my lazy young body, and dancing, and clothes and cars. I assumed that I was intelligent, because I had learned how to bluff. Intellectually I was a lazy zero, even though I had been reading everything from Thomas à Kempis to *The Oz Books* since I was not quite five. I never worried about whether I was good-looking or a decent dancer or an easy learner but simply took all that for granted. (And here I must smile, because my sister Anne and Fay Shoemaker, roommates at Oxy in 1929–30, once almost parted forever because Anne said "for granted" and Fay said "for granite." They argued with fury for long weeks and then did not speak for several more. Who won? Anne died a long time ago, but if I remember I'll ask Fay Shoemaker Powell.) Yes, I took it all for granted/granite!

And as soon as I could escape the trap, whatever it was, I fled family and friends and security like a suddenly freed pigeon, or mole, or wildcat. I probably thought that at last I was MYSELF! And just as probably I would have faltered and even returned with new docility to my cozy cage if I had known how long it would take to start real questioning.

Today, this minute, much more than half a century since I went to Occidental, I begin to understand what I was really learning when I boasted blandly in Dr. Stelter's class about how many books I read each week. Who cared? And when I smugly helped people cheat by doing all their biology drawings for them: what I was really doing was to cheat myself, as I now see it. What about taking for granted that I would get straight A's? I can never be that arrogant again, because now I know how hard many of my peers worked and studied while I played grasshopper. And I know about skin cancers that come from too much sun, and I know about arthritis that stops the heedless endless nights of dancing of both dolts and dukes (or even Counts).

And how about the long process of living with and without people as well as for them, instead of the ignorant pattern of acceptance that for so wasteful a time I believed was the only one for me? Did I start changing all that because I went to Occidental exactly when I did, instead of someplace else some other time? Why do I feel that for undefined reasons I began to look about me there in 1928, instead of in 1924 at the Bishop's School or in 1932 at the University of Dijon?

Who will answer? But I know that it is true, now that I can take the long view.

—1985

About the Author

M.F.K. Fisher was born in Albion, Michigan, in 1908 and spent most of her childhood in Whittier, California. During ensuing years she lived in Dijon, Vevey, Aix-en-Provence, and southern California before moving to the northern California wine country in 1954. She authored over sixteen volumes of essays and reminiscences, including *The Art of Eating, Two Towns in Provence, Among Friends,* and a widely admired translation of Brillat-Savarin's *The Physiology of Taste.* For the last twenty years of her life she lived in a house built for her in Glen Ellen, California. She died at Last House on June 22, 1992.